BLOOM'S ReViews

COMPREHENSIVE RESEARCH & STUDY GUIDES

William Shakespeare's
Hamlet

Edited & with
an Introduction
by Harold Bloom

The Chelsea House World Wide Web site adrress is
http://www.chelseahouse.com

First Printing
1 3 5 7 9 8 6 4 2

Library of Congress Cataloging-in-Publication Data

William Shakespeare's Hamlet / edited and with an introduction by Harold Bloom.
p.   cm.—(Bloom's Notes)
Includes bibliographical references and index.
ISBN 0-7910-3654-5 (hc)   0-7910-4126-3 (pb)
1. Shakespeare, William, 1564–1616. Hamlet. 2. Denmark—In literature.
3. Princes in literature. 4. Tragedy. I. Bloom, Harold. II. Series: Bloom, Harold. Bloom's Notes.
PR2807.W456   1996
822.3'3—dc20
95-13557
CIP
AC

Chelsea House Publishers
1974 Sproul Road, Suite 400
P.O. Box 914
Broomall, PA 19008-0914

Contents

Editor's Note

My Introduction centers upon *Hamlet* as the unique exemplar of Western consciousness, the intellectual as hero or ultimate charismatic personality, akin to the King David of the Bible.

The Critical Views begin with Voltaire's highly ambiguous reaction to Hamlet, followed by Dr. Johnson's curiously reserved reaction to the hero. Goethe's Wilhelm Meister follows with his charming but inaccurate portrayal of Hamlet as a sensitive plant, too pure for this world. More realistically, the German romantic critic August von Schlegel examines the darker elements in Hamlet's character.

English Romantic poet and critic Samuel Taylor Coleridge more properly appreciates Hamlet's intellectuality, which then finds its apotheosis in Nietzsche's celebration of the hero's "insight into the horrible truth" of human existence.

The sublime Oscar Wilde, dramatist and aphorist, follows with a grand appreciation of Hamlet's false friends, the wretched Rosencrantz and Guildenstern. I find Wilde greatly preferable as a *Hamlet* critic to Dr. Sigmund Freud, who suffered from a Hamlet complex and defended himself by falsely judging Hamlet to be an instance of the Oedipus complex.

The great Edwardian critic A. C. Bradley renders a harsh but accurate verdict upon Queen Gertrude, after which we encounter T. S. Eliot's influential but absurd judgment that *Hamlet* is an artistic "failure." Better criticism appears with C. S. Lewis upon Hamlet's monologues, and with Harold Goddard's superb appreciation of Hamlet as a high point in Shakespeare's development.

Terry Eagleton, a British Marxist, reduces Hamlet to an inauthentic exile from society, which is as inauthentic a view as is René Girard's Christianizing of Hamlet's revenge dilemma. I prefer the complex analysis of Joseph H. Summers, who sees that revenge, while un-Christian, nevertheless is ambiguously sanctioned by *Hamlet* as a play.

In a useful reminder, Cedric Watts urges us to keep in mind that Hamlet is a mirror. Thus, we can regard T. McAlindon's sense that love dominates Hamlet, or Zulfikar Ghose's view of Ophelia as a true visionary, as being reflections in critical mirrors, authentic though restricted. This applies also to Kay Stanton's fierce feminist interpretation, which holds that women in *Hamlet* are regarded as whores by all the male characters.

Introduction

HAROLD BLOOM

The largest mistake we can make about the play, *Hamlet,* is to think that it is the tragedy of a man who could not make up his mind, because (presumably) he thinks too much. Though Shakespeare adopts the subgenre of revenge tragedy, his drama has only superficial resemblances to other Elizabethan and Jacobean visions of revenge. The fundamental fact about Hamlet is not that he thinks too much, but that he thinks much too well. His is simply the most intelligent role ever written for the Western stage; indeed, he may be the most intelligent figure in all of world literature, West or East. Unable to rest in illusions of any kind, he thinks his way through to the truth, which may be a pure nihilism, yet a nihilism so purified that it possesses an absolute nobility, even a kind of transcendentalism. At the close Hamlet reasons that, since none of us knows anything about anyone else he leaves behind, what does it matter whether we leave at one time or another? Therefore let it be: the readiness or willingness to depart for that undiscovered country, death, from which no traveler returns, is for the matured Hamlet all in all. The rest is silence.

Shakespeare's longest and most notorious drama, *Hamlet* has imbued four centuries of interpreters with an endless capacity for wonder. We can be spurred to perpetually fresh surmises each time Hamlet speaks, because of a singular element in his consciousness. No other figure in the world's literature seems so much an authorial consciousness in his own right, as though he himself were composing Shakespeare's tragedy. The play itself tells us that he composes a small but significant part of it, by revising *The Murder of Gonzago* (a nonexistent work) into *The Mousetrap,* in order to catch the conscience of the murderous usurper, King Claudius. We do not know exactly which are Hamlet's contributions, but I must think that they include the great speech of the Player-King that concludes:

> Our wills and fates do so contrary run
> That our devices still are overthrown,
> Our thoughts are ours, their ends none of our own.

Freud thought that there were no accidents, so that there was sense in everything, our characters being one with our fates. Hamlet teaches us otherwise, when his Player-King says: "Purpose is but the slave to memory." We find Hamlet's bleak wisdom difficult to absorb, if only because Hamlet is so charismatic a personality, as much so as King David in 2 Samuel or any other secular figure. I use "charismatic" in the sociologist Max Weber's sense: charisma is something that comes from outside the natural sphere, analogous to divine grace, though a displacement of it. Hamlet has an aura about him that never abandons him, even when his feigned madness crosses the line into serious disorder. Shakespeare has a handful of roles almost as intelligent as Hamlet's: Falstaff in the *Henry IV* plays, Portia in *The Merchant of Venice*, Rosalind in *As You Like It*, Cleopatra, and the great villains Iago in *Othello* and Edmund in *King Lear*. But not even Falstaff and Cleopatra have a charisma comparable to Hamlet's. He is beyond us; G. Wilson Knight suggested that Hamlet was death's ambassador to us. Perhaps he is; in Act V, Hamlet speaks with the authority of that undiscovered country, and he hints that he could tell us something crucial if only he had time enough. Death does not permit it, but we receive a hint that the hero's final awareness of eternity is centered in his relation to us, in his concern not to leave a wounded name behind him.

Nietzsche, in the spirit of Hamlet, observed that we only can find words for that which is already dead in our hearts, so that there always is a kind of contempt in the act of speaking. But that is the earlier Hamlet, who seems at least a decade younger than the disinterested sage who returns from the sea to endure the catastrophe of the play's final act. The matured Hamlet who speaks to Horatio has no contempt for expression when he says: "Thou wouldst not think how ill all's here about my heart—." There no longer is a kind of fighting in his heart; the civil war within him has been replaced by intimations of the end. If, as Horatio elegizes, a noble heart cracks with Hamlet's death, we can interpret "noble" in its original sense of "seeing." A seeing heart is Hamlet's final identity, which is very different from the grief-filled, almost traumatized prince whom we encounter as the play opens. Shakespeare, the greatest master of representing changes in the soul, created the most mutable of all his protagonists in Hamlet. Each time that he overhears himself, Hamlet changes, and his radical inwardness continues to augment. Insofar as the history of Western consciousness features a perpetually growing inward self, Hamlet is the central hero of that consciousness.

Some critics have felt that Hamlet is too large a figure even for his own play; that seems to be the true basis for T. S. Eliot's peculiar judgment that his drama was "an aesthetic failure." What, one wonders, is an aesthetic success if *Hamlet* is a failure? And yet, Hamlet does walk out of his play, much as Sir John Falstaff seems to stride out of the two parts of *Henry IV.* Like the Don Quixote and Sancho Panza of Cervantes, Hamlet and Falstaff are universal creations, who stimulate us to envision them in situations and in enterprises not necessarily present in the original texts. Still, the qualities that elevate these four above other literary characters *are* very much present upon the page. In Hamlet's case, it is manifest that revenge is hardly a suitable quest for his greatness, even if revenge were morally less equivocal than it actually is. For so large and exalted a consciousness, one wants a quest comparable in scope to that of Dante the Pilgrim in *The Divine Comedy.* Hamlet palpably is aware of the disproportion between his spirit and the project of revenge; the enigma is why Shakespeare designed his most capacious role as the centerpiece in a domestic tragedy of blood.

A multitude of readers and playgoers, rightly or wrongly, have felt that there must be a very personal relationship between Hamlet and Shakespeare. We know that Shakespeare himself acted the part of the ghost of Hamlet's father when the play was first staged. To think of Hamlet as Shakespeare's son is a very fanciful notion, brilliantly worked out by James Joyce's Stephen Dedalus in the Library scene of *Ulysses.* Shakespeare's only son, Hamnet, whose name differs from Hamlet's by only a single letter, died in 1596 at the age of eleven, less than five years before the play was written. What seems more apposite is A. C. Bradley's observation that Hamlet is the only Shakespearean character who seems capable of writing the play in which he appears. It would be extraordinary if Shakespeare, who imagined Hamlet, had possessed aspects of consciousness left unexplored in Hamlet. Sometimes I entertain another fancy, which is that Hamlet, who uncovers elements of reality that we would not have found for ourselves without him, performed something of the same function for Shakespeare himself. ✤

Biography of William Shakespeare

Few events in the life of William Shakespeare are supported by reliable evidence, and many incidents recorded by commentators of the last four centuries are either conjectural or apocryphal.

William Shakespeare was born in Stratford-upon-Avon on April 22 or 23, 1564, the son of Mary Arden and John Shakespeare, a tradesman. His very early education was in the hands of a tutor, for his parents were probably illiterate. At age seven he entered the Free School in Stratford, where he learned the "small Latin and less Greek" attributed to him by Ben Jonson. When not in school Shakespeare may have gone to the popular Stratford fairs and to the dramas and mystery plays performed by traveling actors.

When Shakespeare was about thirteen his father removed him from school and apprenticed him to a butcher, although it is not known how long he remained in this occupation. When he was eighteen he married Anne Hathaway; their first child, Susanna, was born six months later. A pair of twins, Hamnet and Judith, were born in February 1585. About this time Shakespeare was caught poaching deer on the estate of Sir Thomas Lucy of Charlecot; Lucy's prosecution is said to have inspired Shakespeare to write his earliest literary work, a satire on his opponent. Shakespeare was convicted of poaching and forced to leave Stratford. He withdrew to London, leaving his family behind. He soon attached himself to the stage, initially in a menial capacity (as tender of playgoers' horses, according to one tradition), then as prompter's attendant. When the poaching furor subsided, Shakespeare returned to Stratford to join one of the many bands of itinerant actors. In the next five years he gained what little theater training he received.

By 1592 Shakespeare was a recognized actor, and in that year he wrote and produced his first play, *Henry VI, Part One.* Its success impelled Shakespeare soon afterward to write the second and third parts of *Henry VI.* (Many early and modern

modern critics believe that *Love's Labour's Lost* preceded these histories as Shakespeare's earliest play, but the majority of modern scholars discount this theory.) Shakespeare's popularity provoked the jealousy of Robert Greene, as recorded in his posthumous *Groats-worth of Wit* (1592).

In 1593 Shakespeare published *Venus and Adonis*, a long poem based upon Ovid (or perhaps upon Arthur Golding's translation of Ovid's *Metamorphoses*). It was dedicated to the young Earl of Southampton—but perhaps without permission, a possible indication that Shakespeare was trying to gain the nobleman's patronage. However, the dedicatory address to Southampton in the poem *The Rape of Lucrece* (1594) reveals Shakespeare to have been on good terms with him. Many plays—such as *Titus Andronicus, The Comedy of Errors,* and *Romeo and Juliet*—were produced over the next several years, most performed by Shakespeare's troupe, the Lord Chamberlain's Company. In December 1594 Shakespeare acted in a comedy (of unknown authorship) before Queen Elizabeth; many other royal performances followed in the next decade.

In August 1596 Shakespeare's son Hamnet died. Early the next year Shakespeare bought a home, New Place, in the center of Stratford; he is said to have planted a mulberry tree in the back yard with his own hands. Shakespeare's relative prosperity is indicated by his purchasing more than a hundred acres of farmland in 1602, a cottage near his estate later that year, and half-interest in the tithes of some local villages in 1605.

In September 1598 Shakespeare began his friendship with the then unknown Ben Jonson by producing his play *Every Man in His Humour*. The next year the publisher William Jaggard affixed Shakespeare's name, without his permission, to a curious medley of poems under the title *The Passionate Pilgrim;* the majority of the poems were not by Shakespeare. Two of his sonnets, however, appeared in this collection, although the 154 sonnets, with their mysterious dedication to "Mr. W. H.," were not published as a group until 1609. Also in 1599 the Globe Theatre was built in Southwark (an area of London), and Shakespeare's company began acting there. Many of his greatest plays—*Troilus and Cressida, King Lear, Othello, Macbeth*—were performed in the Globe before its destruction by fire in 1613.

The death in 1603 of Queen Elizabeth, the last of the Tudors, and the accession of James I, from the Stuart dynasty of Scotland, created anxiety throughout England. Shakespeare's fortunes, however, were unaffected, as the new monarch extended the license of Shakespeare's company to perform at the Globe. James I saw a performance of *Othello* at the court in November 1604. In October 1605 Shakespeare's company performed before the Mayor and Corporation of Oxford.

The last five years of Shakespeare's life seem void of incident; he had retired from the stage by 1613. Among the few known incidents is Shakespeare's involvement in a heated and lengthy dispute about the enclosure of common-fields around Stratford. He died on April 23, 1616, and was buried in the Church of St. Mary's in Stratford. A monument was later erected to him in the Poets' Corner of Westminster Abbey.

Numerous corrupt quarto editions of Shakespeare's plays were published during his lifetime. These editions, based either on manuscripts, prompt-books, or sometimes merely actors' recollections of the plays, were meant to capitalize on Shakespeare's renown. Other plays, now deemed wholly or largely spurious—*Edward the Third, The Yorkshire Tragedy, The Two Noble Kinsmen,* and others—were also published under Shakespeare's name during and after his lifetime. Shakespeare's plays were collected in the First Folio of 1623 by John Heminge and Henry Condell. Nine years later the Second Folio was published, and in 1640 Shakespeare's poems were collected. The first standard collected edition was by Nicholas Rowe (1709), followed by the editions of Alexander Pope (1723–25), Lewis Theobald (1733), Samuel Johnson (1765), Edmond Malone (1790), and many others.

Shakespeare's plays are now customarily divided into the following categories (probable dates of writing are given in brackets): comedies (*The Comedy of Errors* [1590], *The Taming of the Shrew* [1592], *The Two Gentlemen of Verona* [1592–93], *A Midsummer Night's Dream* [1595], *Love's Labour's Lost* [1595], *The Merchant of Venice* [1596–98], *As You Like It* [1597], *The Merry Wives of Windsor* [1597], *Much Ado About Nothing* [1598–99], *Twelfth Night* [1601], *All's Well That Ends Well* [1603–04], and *Measure for Measure* [1604]); histories

(*Henry the Sixth, Part One* [1590–92], *Henry the Sixth, Parts Two and Three* [1590–92], *Richard the Third* [1591], *King John* [1591–98], *Richard the Second* [1595], *Henry the Fourth, Part One* [1597], *Henry the Fourth, Part Two* [1597], *Henry the Fifth* [1599], and *Henry the Eighth* [1613]); tragedies (*Titus Andronicus* [1590], *Romeo and Juliet* [1595], *Julius Caesar* [1599], *Hamlet* [1599–1601], *Troilus and Cressida* [1602], *Othello* [1602–04], *King Lear* [1604–05], *Macbeth* [1606], *Timon of Athens* [1607], *Antony and Cleopatra* [1606–07], and *Coriolanus* [1608]); romances (*Pericles, Prince of Tyre* [1606–08], *Cymbeline* [1609–10], *The Winter's Tale* [1610–11], and *The Tempest* [1611]). However, Shakespeare willfully defied the canons of classical drama by mingling comedy, tragedy, and history, so that in some cases classification is debatable or arbitrary.

Shakespeare's reputation, while subject to many fluctuations, was firmly established by the eighteenth century. Samuel Johnson remarked: "Perhaps it would not be easy to find any authour, except Homer, who invented so much as Shakespeare, who so much advanced the studies which he cultivated, who effused so much novelty upon his age or country. The form, the characters, the language, and the shows of the English drama are his." Early in the nineteenth century Samuel Taylor Coleridge declared: "The Englishman who without reverence, a proud and affectionate reverence, can utter the name of William Shakespeare, stands disqualified for the office of critic. . . . Great as was the genius of Shakespeare, his judgment was at least equal to it."

A curious controversy developed in the middle of the nineteenth century in regard to the authorship of Shakespeare's plays, some contending that Sir Francis Bacon was the actual author of the plays, others (including Mark Twain) advancing the claims of the Earl of Oxford. None of these attempts has succeeded in persuading the majority of scholars that Shakespeare himself is not the author of the plays attributed to him.

In recent years many landmark editions of Shakespeare, with increasingly accurate texts and astute critical commentary, have emerged. These include the New Cambridge Shakespeare

(1984 f.) and the New Arden Shakespeare (1951f.). Such critics as T. S. Eliot, G. Wilson Knight, Northrop Frye, W. H. Auden, and many others have continued to elucidate Shakespeare, his work, and his times, and he remains the most written-about author in the history of English literature. ❖

Thematic and Structural Analysis

The Tragedy of Hamlet, Prince of Denmark opens on a note of darkness and suspicion, as nervous sentinels cross paths during the night's watch. These guards are joined by Hamlet's confidant, Horatio, and we learn that they have an excellent reason to be jumpy: For the past two nights their watch has been visited by a ghostly apparition in the form of old Hamlet—the recently deceased father of the prince that bears his name. The skeptical Horatio has come to see if the vision will reappear, which it does, crossing the stage quickly and ignoring Horatio's attempts to speak with it.

Horatio interprets the apparition as an omen of political catastrophe. For, as the play opens, Denmark is also endangered by the prospect of an attack by an army of Norwegian brigands under the command of young Fortinbras. Years before the time of the play, the old king Hamlet had killed Fortinbras's father (who was then king of Norway) in single combat, and by doing so won possession of Norwegian lands. Now, Fortinbras is preparing an army to reconquer the territory his father lost. As Horatio and the guards are discussing the possible relationship between the threat of Fortinbras and the apparition of the ghost, the latter reappears. Again Horatio attempts to speak with it, but this time a rooster's crow announces the coming of day and the ghost departs without responding. It is decided that young Hamlet should accompany the watch on the following evening.

From this opening scene of darkness and terror, the play moves to a scene of public, ceremonial grandeur at the Danish court (**Act I, scene 2**). The sharp contrast is typical of Shakespearean stagecraft: While the confidence and formality of the court language may give the impression of a well-run and orderly state, the audience still remembers the ominous mood established by the previous scene. This second scene opens with King Claudius performing the public offices of kingship. He acknowledges the community's grief at the passing of old Hamlet (who we learn was Claudius's brother), gracefully alludes to his own marriage to old Hamlet's widow, Gertrude, and thanks the assembly for their support. He then sends ambassadors to Fortinbras's uncle, the current king of Norway, asking him to curtail his nephew's warlike ambition. Finally, as befits a king, Claudius listens to his subjects' suits: young Laertes (with the support of his father, Polonius) asks leave to travel to France, which Claudius graciously grants.

With this, Claudius turns to address young Hamlet, who has recently returned from his studies in Wittenburg in order to attend the funeral of his father and the wedding of his newly widowed mother to Claudius. From his first appearance, Hamlet stands out: he is the sole figure on the crowded stage dressed entirely in funeral black; his language, instead of being ceremonial and formal, is full of puns and double entendres; he lashes out bitterly and openly at what he sees as the superficiality of court ceremony. Claudius and Gertrude both ask Hamlet to remain in Denmark, and he agrees to do so. The court departs, leaving Hamlet alone on stage, and he delivers the first of the four great soliloquies that punctuate the play.

Since the play's central puzzles involve the relationship between Hamlet's inner life and his public actions, these soliloquies—in which we get a glimpse of Hamlet's private thoughts—are of the utmost importance. Here, we learn that Hamlet saw his late father as a paragon, an almost godlike man. However, Hamlet's most powerful emotions here seem to be directed at his mother: revulsion at her remarriage and incredulity at her willingness to settle for Claudius after having loved old Hamlet. In fact, his disgust for his mother's actions lead him to lash out at women in general: "Frailty, thy name is woman." Horatio appears with news of the ghost, and Hamlet agrees to join the watch at the appointed time.

In **Act I, scene 3,** the play joins young Laertes as he is about to depart for France. Like a dutiful brother, he offers advice to his sister, Ophelia, who has been receiving overtures of love from Hamlet. Their father, Polonius, fearing that his daughter's chastity may be compromised, orders Ophelia to cut off all communication with the prince.

Night falls, and Hamlet and Horatio join the sentinels in their watch (**I.4**). To Hamlet's considerable astonishment, the ghost reappears and beckons to him. Though the others try to dissuade him, Hamlet feels compelled to follow the ghost regardless of the danger. Alone with Hamlet, the apparition announces that he is in fact the spirit of old Hamlet, and describes—in graphic and intense language—how his brother Claudius first murdered him by pouring poison in his ear, and then seduced his wife (**I.5**). Moreover, since old Hamlet was murdered while sleeping, he never had a chance to receive absolution for his earthly sins and has suffered terrible torments in purgatory. Old Hamlet gives his son a specific set of commands: avenge the murder by killing Claudius, but do not harm Gertrude—and departs, calling "adieu, adieu, adieu. Remember me." The ghost's account strikes a chord in Hamlet, for it confirms his sense that his mother's hasty remarriage was wrong, and gives shape to the resentment he had already felt toward Claudius. He vows passionately to fulfill his father's request, promising never to be distracted from his vengeful purpose. Rejoined by Horatio and a guard, Hamlet greets them excitedly but refuses to tell them what has taken place. Hamlet asks his companions three times to swear never to reveal what they have seen; each time the voice of the ghost echoes "swear" from below the stage, and each time, they swear to keep silent. Hamlet also intimates that he may find it necessary to behave oddly—to "put an antic disposition on"—and requests that his companions never take his behavior amiss or attempt to explain it to anyone.

At the start of **Act II,** Ophelia reports to her father that she has seen Hamlet, and that he is in physical and emotional disarray. Polonius—who, after all, has just forbidden Ophelia to see the prince—interprets Hamlet's distress as lovesickness, and goes off to inform the king. He arrives at the court (**II.2**) to find Claudius with Rosencrantz and Guildenstern, two friends of Hamlet's from school, whom the king has summoned in hopes that they might discover the root of Hamlet's sadness. As Polonius prepares to offer his interpretation of Hamlet's behavior, he is interrupted by the arrival of the ambassador from Norway, who brings good news: Fortinbras's plan has been curtailed by the Norwegian king; instead of attacking Denmark, Fortinbras proposes to attack Poland with his assembled troops, and requests permission to pass peaceably through

Denmark to do so. Once the ambassador has gone, Polonius shows the king and queen one of Hamlet's love letters to Ophelia, and suggests that he may have been driven mad by love.

Hamlet approaches, and the king and queen depart. Polonius attempts to make small talk with Hamlet, but the prince puts him off with a series of odd, tangential remarks, many of which have lewd or grotesque double meanings. Polonius recognizes that there is method in Hamlet's madness, but interprets the exchange as support for his theory that Hamlet has been driven mad by love for Ophelia. In this scene, as in similar scenes throughout the remainder of the play, it is impossible for the audience to know how much of Hamlet's behavior can be attributed to the "antic disposition" he has decided to put on, and how much of it expresses his real obsessions. Certainly, the offhand remarks that Hamlet directs at the play's other characters return obsessively to the interconnected themes of sexuality, birth, and death. Moreover, it is easy to recognize that there might be a connection between these themes and Hamlet's deep feelings about the mother that bore him and the murder of his father. Indeed, the play invites psychological speculation, though it provides no easy answers to the puzzle of Hamlet's mental makeup.

Polonius departs, and Hamlet is joined by Rosencrantz and Guildenstern. After some typically bawdy banter, Hamlet forces them to admit that they were sent for by Claudius. Rosencrantz and Guildenstern tell Hamlet that a troupe of actors is due at the palace, and the prince seems to take a real interest—asking informed questions and dropping for the moment his antic manner. He also confides to Rosencrantz and Guildenstern that his odd behavior is a ruse. When the actors arrive, Hamlet welcomes them warmly, and joins them in reciting passages from plays.

At this point, one begins to wonder why Hamlet's revenge is taking so long to develop. Despite his vow to execute swift vengeance, Hamlet has not yet done anything to further a plan. It turns out that Hamlet himself is wondering the same thing, for in the second of his soliloquies he contrasts the passion of the actors with his own inability to launch a plan for sudden revenge. Seemingly unable to understand his own inaction, Hamlet rebukes himself for being too thoughtful and too wordy:

Promped to revenge (handwritten)

> Why, what an ass am I! This is most brave,
> That I, the son of a dear father murder'd
> Prompted to my revenge by heaven and hell
> Must like a whore unpack my heart with words. . . .

The word "prompted" is suggestive here, for it is itself a word from the theatre: An actor gets a prompt when he has forgotten his line. Elsewhere in this same speech, Hamlet describes his father's command as his "cue" to action. The implication is that though Hamlet knows what he is supposed to do, he feels like an actor preparing for a role rather than like an outraged son. Simply put, Hamlet feels that he lacks the passion to commit a rash murder.

Toward the end of this soliloquy it occurs to Hamlet that the ghost may have been lying, since after all the devil can assume "a pleasing shape." Hamlet's concern here can be interpreted either as a genuine moral scruple or as an attempt to justify his continued inaction. Either way, Hamlet decides to test the ghost's story by asking the players to enact a murder resembling old Hamlet's in a play put on before the court. If Claudius acts guilty when he sees his own treachery staged, then the ghost's story can be believed.

At the beginning of **Act III,** we find Claudius and his court actively attempting to solve the problems presented by Hamlet's behavior. Rosencrantz and Guildenstern inform Claudius that though they have been unable to get to the bottom of Hamlet's melancholy, the prince has at least expressed an interest in the actors and has in fact requested the presence of the king at one of their productions. Polonius attempts to set up a meeting between Ophelia and Hamlet so that he and Claudius may spy on them. Here the audience also gets its first clear indication of Claudius's guilt, for when Polonius makes an offhand remark about deceit, the king has an aside in which he exclaims "How smart a lash that speech doth give my conscience." Polonius and Claudius withdraw, and Hamlet enters for his third soliloquy.

This speech ("To be, or not to be") may well be the single most recognizable passage in all English literature. Remarkably, instead of addressing the immediate issue at hand, Hamlet's thoughts here run to the highest and most abstract questions: Is it better to live with suffering, or to die and take one's chances on an unknown afterlife? If we do not know what will happen after death, how can we ever know how to act properly during life? These questions bear on Hamlet's situation in a number of ways. He may be contemplating suicide—as he seems also to do briefly in his first soliloquy. One could also argue that he is wondering about the ultimate morality of revenge here. After all, Hamlet has learned that even his beloved father—an ideal man—has been subject to unspeakable torments in purgatory. With the idea of his father's guilt fresh in his mind, Hamlet may justifiably be worried about precisely this kind of moral question. Alternatively, he may be exploring more generally his own inability to find any certain basis for purposeful human action: if life is fleeting and insignificant, how can any human actions be worth caring about. All these thoughts seem to be mixed together in this famous soliloquy, but their respective importance, and their relevance to Hamlet's immediate situation, are left as puzzles for the audience.

Ophelia enters, interrupting Hamlet's musings. Though he speaks kindly of her as she approaches, Hamlet's conversation with her verges on cruelty. He asserts that all women are promiscuous, tells Ophelia that he can no longer love her, and calls for an end to the institution of marriage. Again, it is tempting to relate Hamlet's attacks on women generally to his feelings about his mother's remarriage. Baffled by his unexpected tirades, Ophelia can only conclude that Hamlet has gone mad. Claudius and Polonius, who have been spying on the couple, disagree in their interpretations of Hamlet's behavior. Polonius still thinks it has its origins in love, while Claudius thinks it must be something else, and begins to ponder sending Hamlet to England for a change of scenery.

Act III, scene 2 begins with Hamlet giving last-minute theatrical advice to the actors, who are about to put his plan into effect. Claudius and his court assemble to see the play—in

Hamlet In Purgatory

which a king is murdered by a nephew who pours poison in his ear—and Hamlet's scheme works to perfection. The king is startled by the resemblance between the play and his own crime. When the murder is committed on stage, he calls out for light and puts an abrupt end to the performance. The crowd disperses, leaving Hamlet and Horatio to mull over the king's guilty response, until Rosencrantz and Guildenstern arrive to inform Hamlet that the king is not feeling well, and that Gertrude would like to see him in her chamber. Polonius enters and reiterates this message.

Act III, scene 3 opens with Claudius urging Rosencrantz and Guildenstern to take Hamlet to England at once. Polonius tells the king that Hamlet is headed to his mother's chamber, and promises to spy on their meeting by hiding behind a tapestry hanging from the wall. Left alone, Claudius kneels down and attempts to pray, but finds that his guilty conscience will not allow him even that peace. Hamlet enters, finds the king alone, and immediately recognizes that he has been given a perfect opportunity to exact the revenge promised to the ghost. Hamlet decides to let the king live, however. He decides that if he kills Claudius at prayer, the latter will have had an opportunity to purge his sins. Since old Hamlet was given no such opportunity, this murder would not be a fit revenge. Hamlet's decision here can be seen in two ways: either it is a manifestation of extreme cruelty—he wants Claudius not only to die but to suffer eternal damnation for his sins—or it is a rationalization justifying Hamlet's inability to commit cold-blooded murder.

In **Act III, scene 4,** Hamlet shows that he is capable of a different kind of murder. He arrives at his mother's chamber, hears Polonius scuffling behind the tapestry, and stabs him to death. Then, virtually ignoring the dead body of Polonius, Hamlet berates his mother for marrying Claudius. The emotional intensity with which Hamlet chides his mother is unmistakable, and his speeches manifest a powerful physical disgust at the thought of his mother's sexual interest in Claudius. During this exchange, the ghost reappears to sharpen Hamlet's "blunted purpose" and to drive him toward the revenge he has inexplicably put off. Gertrude cannot see the ghost (one wonders why, since Horatio and the others did in the first act), and is convinced of Hamlet's madness. She appears to be chastened by his accusations, though we cannot tell if her response is sincere. She may simply be playing along with what she perceives to be Hamlet's terrifying madness. Pleased with his mother's change of heart, Hamlet departs, dragging the dead body of Polonius behind him.

In **Act IV, scene 1,** Gertrude describes Hamlet's madness to Claudius, and reports the death of Polonius. The king immediately sends Rosencrantz and Guildenstern after Hamlet, hoping that they will be able at least to find the old man's body. They come upon Hamlet just as he has "stowed" the corpse (**IV.2**),. and Hamlet is openly scornful of their attempts to question him. Hamlet faces Claudius in **scene 3,** maintaining his antic manner, musing on the universality of death and on the meaninglessness of social rank.. The king hurriedly dispatches Hamlet (along with Rosencrantz and Guildenstern) to England, along with letters addressed to the English king ordering Hamlet's execution.

Act IV, scene 4 finds Hamlet and his escorts heading toward the coast, where they encounter Fortinbras and his army. By talking to a captain, Hamlet discovers that the army is marching toward Poland, impelled by honor to do battle over a truly worthless plot of ground. Astonished that so many men should risk their lives for so little, Hamlet tells his escorts to go ahead and delivers his fourth and final soliloquy. In it, he contrasts his own inability to kill Claudius with the senseless bravery of all these thousands of troops. Greatness, he concludes, lies in the capacity to care deeply over even trifles when honor is at stake. Seeing that he has not been able to muster this kind of passionate concern, he rededicates himself yet again to "bloody" thoughts.

Act IV, scene 5 shows the aftereffects of Polonius's death. Ophelia goes mad with grief, and her madness takes the form of an extreme and touching flightiness. She wanders in and out of the scene singing snatches of ballads and speaking in poignantly nonsensical fragments. Laertes, meanwhile, returns from France, gathers a mob of supporters, and threatens to stop at nothing to avenge his father's death. In a fury, he storms Claudius's castle, where the king is able to calm him somewhat by promising to help him get to the bottom of Polonius's death.

We might note here that Laertes's passionate anger is precisely what Hamlet has been hitherto unable to generate. Indeed, many of Laertes's angry exclamations here seem designed specifically to highlight the contrast between the two characters. We should notice that Hamlet's failure to exact revenge stands in marked contrast to both Fortinbras and Laertes. Each of the sons in this play is put in a position to avenge his father's death. Though his plans are thwarted, Fortinbras at least wants to recapture the lands his great father lost, and Laertes's desire for vengeance is virtually irrepressible. Only Hamlet finds it difficult to act, which makes his hesitation stand out conspicuously in the world of the play.

At this point **(IV.6)** a sailor arrives, bearing a letter from Hamlet to Horatio. It seems that the ship bound for England has been attacked by pirates, and that only Hamlet was captured. In return for some undisclosed ransom or service, the pirates have deposited Hamlet on his native soil. Hamlet's letter also alludes to some secrets (presumably Claudius's villainy), and bids Horatio come to him at once. The king is trying to placate Laertes in **scene 7**, explaining that Hamlet is too dear to his mother and too popular with the Danish people to be prosecuted openly for Polonius's murder. He is in the process of describing Hamlet's expected execution in England when a messenger appears with a letter from Hamlet, and news that the prince has returned safely to Denmark.

Laertes wants to slaughter Hamlet at once, but Claudius gets him to participate in a craftier plan. The king reveals that Hamlet has always had a jealous admiration for Laertes's prowess with swords, and argues, consequently, that if Laertes were to challenge the prince to a fencing match, his challenge would certainly be accepted. In such a match, Claudius suggests, it would be easy enough to kill Hamlet without creating a public disturbance. Laertes answers that he has some deadly poison with which he will anoint his rapier, and Claudius adds that he will have a chalice full of poisoned wine ready to serve to the prince as a toast between rounds. That way, even if Laertes fails, Hamlet will die. As they finalize these plans,

Gertrude enters and—in a touchingly lyrical speech—reports that Ophelia has drowned.

Act V begins in a graveyard, as a grave-digger and another man prepare Ophelia's grave. Hamlet and Horatio enter, unaware that the grave being readied is for Ophelia. Among the skulls strewn about the graveyard, Hamlet finds the skull of Yorick, Old Hamlet's jester, also Hamlet's beloved childhood playmate. In one of Shakepeare's most famous and moving speeches, Hamlet reflects on how all earthly distinctions of social class and individual accomplishment disappear in death. Everyone–no matter how well-loved or revered–ends up as a mere heap of bones, virtually indistinguishable from all the rest. He can only conclude that scale of human endeavor is miniscule in the grand scheme of things. Hamlet's reverie is interrupted with the arrival of Ophelia's funeral party, and he is startled to discover that the grave he has been haunting is hers. Laertes laments wildly over his sister's body, leaps into her grave, and demands to be buried alongside her. Something in Laertes's manner–proof that he has the passion Hamlet lacks?—provokes Hamlet's feelings of rivalry. He leaps into the grave beside Laertes and attempts to outdo him in the expression of sorrow. Claudius barely keeps the situation under control, asking Horatio to look after his friend, and reminding Laertes to be patient.

The final scene (**V.2**) begins as Hamlet tells Horatio about his experiences at sea: after stealing Claudius's letter to the king of England from Rosencrantz and Guildenstern, Hamlet replaced it with a forged letter ordering the pair's immediate execution. Hamlet and Horatio are then joined by a foppish young courtier named Osric who announces that the king has wagered on Hamlet in a fencing match with Laertes. Despite a foreboding premonition, Hamlet agrees to participate in the competition, and preparations for the match are hurriedly made. As Hamlet and Laertes square off, the prince apologizes. Laertes accepts the apology, but stiffly responds that he cannot be fully reconciled until honor is satisfied. The match begins auspiciously for Hamlet, who strikes Laertes twice, but swiftly devolves into a bloodbath. Gertrude drinks the poisoned wine over the feeble protestations of her husband; Laertes stabs Hamlet with the poison rapier; in a scuffle, the two men exchange rapiers, and Hamlet inadvertently poisons Laertes by striking him. Gertrude dies, and Laertes—who knows that he and Hamlet have both been poisoned—confesses and implicates the king. Hamlet stabs Claudius with the poisoned blade and then forces him to drink the dregs of the poisoned wine. Though Hamlet finally avenges his father's murder here, the murder is almost an afterthought: even the rapier with which he finally kills the king is literally put into his hand by accident. Hamlet never generates the kind of purposeful passion displayed by Laertes and expected of him by his father's ghost.

The king dies. Laertes dies. Hamlet, in his death throes, implores Horatio to report truly all that has taken place. Hamlet's final act is to name Fortinbras the new king of Denmark. As if on cue, Fortinbras arrives on his way back from Poland. Tying up the last loose end, an ambassador arrives from England with news that Rosencrantz and Guildenstern have been executed. Horatio promises to tell the tale of Hamlet "to th' yet unknowing world," and as the play comes to a close, Fortinbras orders his soldiers to prepare a military funeral for Hamlet.

Revenge plots were common when Shakespeare wrote *Hamlet*. What sets this play apart is its emphasis on character, for it is precisely Hamlet's inaction—his apparent inability to execute the kind of rash killing required of him by the ghost— that becomes the central point of interest. There is much in the figure of Hamlet to speculate on: from the enormously rich range of ideas and concerns that enter into his soliloquies to the recurring obsession with sex and death that seems to underlie his antic remarks in public to his conflicting feelings about his mother, father, and uncle. Much about the character remains stubbornly enigmatic, and the audience is left to answer several key questions: What exactly is Hamlet's mental state, and why does it impede his revenge? Does the character develop or change over the course of the play? And so on. Even Hamlet's final words seem calculated to underscore his enigmatic quality: "The rest is silence." ❖

—*Curtis Perry*
Harvard University

List of Characters

Hamlet, prince of Denmark, is the principal character of the play. Though a speech by the gravedigger (5.1) pinpoints Hamlet's age at thirty, there is reason elsewhere to believe that he may be younger: he is a student, and the peer of a generation (including Laertes and Fortinbras) that is only beginning to come into its own. Returning to Denmark to attend the funeral of his father the king and the remarriage of his mother to Claudius, Hamlet is visited by the ghost of his father. The ghost relates how he was murdered by Claudius, and commands Hamlet to seek revenge. Hamlet vows to do so. Much of the play is spent exploring Hamlet's complicated frame of mind in the period of time between his promise to the ghost and his murder of Claudius in the play's final scene.

Old Hamlet is Hamlet's father, who was king of Denmark until being murdered by Claudius in the prehistory of the play. His ghost haunts the play, commanding Hamlet to avenge the murder. Old Hamlet was apparently a powerful warrior in his day, having both defeated Poland and bested the king of Norway in single combat. Old Hamlet occupies a special place in his son's imagination. Hamlet repeatedly describes him as an ideal of manhood, a representative of a heroic age that may be irretrievably lost.

Gertrude is Hamlet's mother, the widow of old Hamlet, and the wife of Claudius. Though we know that she dotes upon her son, we do not know how she feels about her first husband, her relation to her second husband's guilt, or her son's accusations. Though she herself is only sketchily presented, she plays a major role in Hamlet's inner life: on several occasions he bitterly complains of her failure to honor old Hamlet's memory, and his ambivalence about her seems to color his response to Ophelia. Gertrude is accidentally killed at the end of the play, when she drinks poison intended for her son.

Claudius, Hamlet's uncle, becomes king of Denmark by killing old Hamlet and marrying his widow. Though troubled by a guilty conscience and provoked to further villainy by Hamlet's antisocial behavior, Claudius attempts throughout to maintain public order in Denmark. After plotting with Laertes to poison

Hamlet during a fencing match, Claudius is killed by the poison intended for the prince.

Horatio is Hamlet's friend and confidant. Horatio, like Hamlet, has studied at Wittenburg: he is presented as learned and reliable, though lacking the prince's imaginative brilliance. Horatio assists Hamlet throughout the play. As Hamlet dies, he makes Horatio promise to report truly on all that has taken place.

Polonius is father of Laertes and Ophelia, and adviser to Claudius. He is represented as a comically sententious, nosy old man, and as the dispenser of long-winded and clichéd advice. His nosiness proves to be his undoing: in service to the king, he hides behind a tapestry to eavesdrop when Hamlet visits his mother; Hamlet hears him, and stabs him to death. Polonius's death drives Ophelia mad, provokes in Laertes a murderous rage for vengeance, and convinces Claudius that Hamlet must be sent to England and quietly executed.

Ophelia is sister to Laertes and daughter to Polonius. Though Hamlet has been courting her, Ophelia willingly obeys her father when he tells her to discourage the prince's advances. Later, she bears the brunt of Hamlet's acerbic cynicism on more than one occasion. When Polonius is killed, she is driven mad and accidentally drowns herself. Ophelia is presented throughout the play as loving, innocent, and obedient. Victimized by the play's tragic actions, her madness and subsequent death are rendered poignantly and are fully undeserved.

Laertes is the son of Polonius and brother of Ophelia. At the start of the play Laertes leaves for France, but returns in a rage at the news of his father's death. Laertes is presented throughout the play as Hamlet's peer, rival, and counterpart. His passionate desire to avenge his father's murder stands in marked contrast to Hamlet's inaction. In the carnage of the final scene, Laertes kills—and is in turn killed by—Hamlet.

Fortinbras is the son of the late king of Norway. He is also the leader of an army of "lawless resolutes" with which, as the play begins, he plans to recapture the lands that old Hamlet won from his father in single combat. The king of Norway forbids the attack, and Fortinbras leads his troops into Poland instead. Like Laertes, Fortinbras functions in the play as a foil for Hamlet, for his desire to attack Denmark is also an attempt to avenge his father's death at the hands of old Hamlet. Fortinbras and his army enter the Danish court during the play's final scene, just as Hamlet, Laertes, Claudius, and Gertrude are dying. With the support of the dying prince, Fortinbras assumes the mantle of authority in Denmark.

Rosencrantz and Guildenstern are old friends of Hamlet's and would-be courtiers summoned by Claudius and Gertrude to discover the root of Hamlet's melancholy. Hamlet's treatment of them goes from friendly to scornful as it becomes increasingly clear that they are motivated only by their interest in the king's favor. Claudius sends them with Hamlet to England, and orders them to deliver his letters to the English king. These letters contain orders for Hamlet's execution, though it is not clear that Rosencrantz and Guildenstern know this. Hamlet steals the letters from them, and replaces them with a forged letter ordering their execution instead. As the play ends, ambassadors from England arrive with news that the pair have been killed. ❖

Critical Views

[Voltaire was the pseudonym of François Marie Arouet (1694–1778), one of the most noted French philosophers, novelists, and historians of the eighteenth century and author of *Candide* (1759). Voltaire, although objecting violently to Shakespeare's defiance of the dramatic "unities" (the notion—derived from a false conception of ancient Greek tragedy—that plays should take place in only one locale and within a very restricted period of time), found *Hamlet* a powerfully moving play, especially in the awesome spectacle of the ghost of Hamlet's father.]

The Roman philosophers had no faith in ghosts in the time of the emperors, and yet young Pompey raises one in the *Pharsalia.* The English have certainly no more belief in spirits than the Romans had, and yet they see every day with pleasure, in the tragedy of *Hamlet,* the ghost of a king, who appears nearly the same as the apparition of Ninus did at Paris. I am at the same time far from justifying the tragedy of *Hamlet* in every respect; it is a gross and barbarous piece, and would never be borne by the lowest of the rabble in France or Italy. Hamlet runs mad in the second act, and his mistress in the third; the prince kills the father of his mistress and fancies he is killing a rat; and the heroine of the play throws herself into the river. They dig her grave on the stage, and the grave-diggers, holding the dead men's skulls in their hands, talk nonsense worthy of them. Hamlet answers their abominable stuff by some whimsies not less disgusting; during this time one of the actors makes the conquest of Poland. Hamlet, his mother, and father-in-law, drink together on the stage: they sing at table, quarrel, beat and kill one another; one would think the whole piece was the product of the imagination of a drunken savage: and yet, among all these gross irregularities, which make the English theatre even at this day so absurd and barbarous, we find in *Hamlet,* which is still more strange and unaccountable, some sublime strokes worthy of the greatest genius. It seems as if nature took pleasure to unite in the head of Shakespeare all that we can imagine great and forcible, together with all that the grossest dullness could produce of everything that is most low and detestable.

It must be acknowledged, that, among the beauties that shine forth in the midst of all these horrid extravagancies, the ghost of Hamlet's father is one of the most striking: it has always a strong effect on the English—I mean, on those who are the best judges and are most hurt by the irregularity of their old theatre. This ghost inspires more terror, even in the reading, than the apparition of Darius in the *Persians* of Æschylus: and why does it? because Darius, in Æschylus, only appears to foretell the misfortunes of his family; whereas, in Shakespeare, the ghost of Hamlet appears to demand vengeance, and to reveal secret crimes. It is neither useless, nor brought in by force, but serves to convince mankind, that there is an invisible power, the master of nature. All men have a sense of justice imprinted on their hearts, and naturally wish that heaven would interest itself in the cause of innocence: in every age, therefore, and in every nation, they will behold with pleasure, the Supreme Being engaged in the punishment of crimes which could not come within the reach of human laws: this is a consolation to the weak, and a restraint on the insolence and obstinacy of the powerful.

> Heaven
> Will oft suspend its own eternal laws
> When justice calls, reversing death's decree,
> Thus to chastise the sovereigns of the earth,
> And terrify mankind—

Thus Semiramis speaks to the high priest of Babylon, and thus the successor of Samuel might have spoken to Saul, when the ghost of Samuel came to tell him of his condemnation.

I will go still further, and venture to affirm, when an extraordinary circumstance of this kind is mentioned in the beginning of a tragedy, when it is properly prepared, when things are so situated as to render it necessary and even looked for and desired by the spectators; it ought then to be considered as perfectly natural: it is at the same time sufficiently obvious, that these bold strokes are not to be too often repeated.

—François Marie Arouet (Voltaire), "Ancient and Modern Tragedy" (1749), *Works,* tr. William F. Fleming (Paris: E. R. Du Mont, 1901), Vol. 19, pp. 136–38

SAMUEL JOHNSON ON "TO BE OR NOT TO BE"

[Samuel Johnson (1709–1784), perhaps the greatest British literary figure of the eighteenth century, was a poet, novelist, critic, and biographer of distinction. In 1765 he wrote a monograph, *Preface to His Edition of Shakespeare,* and in that same year he edited a land- mark annotated edition of Shakespeare's works, still highly regarded for the astuteness of its commentary. In this extract, taken from the notes to his edition, Johnson finds many flaws in *Hamlet* and also devotes considerable attention to a close reading of Hamlet's famous soliloquy beginning, "To be or not to be . . ."]

If the dramas of Shakespeare were to be characterised, each by the particular excellence which distinguishes it from the rest, we must allow to the tragedy of *Hamlet* the praise of variety. The incidents are so numerous, that the argument of the play would make a long tale. The scenes are interchangeably diver- sified with merriment and solemnity; with merriment that includes judicious and instructive observations, and solemnity, not strained by poetical violence above the natural sentiments of man. New characters appear from time to time in continual succession, exhibiting various forms of life and particular modes of conversation. The pretended madness of Hamlet causes much mirth, the mournful distraction of Ophelia fills the heart with tenderness, and every personage produces the effect intended, from the apparition that in the first act chills the blood with horror, to the fop in the last, that exposes affec- tation to just contempt.

The conduct is perhaps not wholly secure against objections. The action is indeed for the most part in continual progression, but there are some scenes which neither forward nor retard it. Of the feigned madness of Hamlet there appears no adequate cause, for he does nothing which he might not have done with the reputation of sanity. He plays the madman most, when he treats Ophelia with so much rudeness, which seems to be useless and wanton cruelty.

Hamlet is, through the whole play, rather an instrument than an agent. After he has, by the stratagem of the play, convicted the King, he makes no attempt to punish him, and his death is at last effected by an incident which Hamlet has no part in producing.

The catastrophe is not very happily produced; the exchange of weapons is rather an expedient of necessity, than a stroke of art. A scheme might easily have been formed, to kill Hamlet with the dagger, and Laertes with the bowl.

The poet is accused of having shewn little regard to poetical justice, and may be charged with equal neglect of poetical probability. The apparition left the regions of the dead to little purpose; the revenge which he demands is not obtained but by the death of him that was required to take it; and the gratification which would arise from the destruction of an usurper and a murderer, is abated by the untimely death of Ophelia, the young, the beautiful, the harmless, and the pious. ⟨. . .⟩

Of ⟨Hamlet's⟩ celebrated soliloquy, which bursting from a man distracted with contrariety of desires, and overwhelmed with the magnitude of his own purposes, is connnected rather in the speaker's mind, than on his tongue, I shall endeavour to discover the train, and to shew how one sentiment produces another.

Hamlet, knowing himself injured in the most enormous and atrocious degree, and seeing no means of redress, but such as must expose him to the extremity of hazard, meditates on his situation in this manner: "Before I can form any rational scheme of action under this pressure of distress," it is necessary to decide whether, "after our present state, we are *to be or not to be.*" That is the question, which, as it shall be answered, will determine, "whether 'tis nobler," and more suitable to the dignity of reason, "to suffer the outrages of fortune" patiently, or to take arms against, "them," and by opposing end them, "though perhaps" with the loss of life. If "to die," were "to sleep, no more, and by a sleep to end" the miseries of our nature, such a sleep were "devoutly to be wished"; but if "to sleep" in death, be "to dream," to retain our powers of sensibility, we must "pause" to consider, "in that sleep of death what dreams may come." This consideration "makes calamity" so long endured; "for who would bear" the vexations of life, which might be ended "by a bare bodkin," but that he is afraid of something in unknown futurity? This fear it is that gives efficacy to conscience, which, by turning the mind upon "this regard," chills the ardour of "resolution," checks the vigour of "enterprise," and makes the "current" to desire stagnate in inactivity.

—Samuel Johnson, *The Plays of William Shakespeare* (London: J. & R. Tonson, 1765), Vol. 8, pp. 311, 207

JOHANN WOLFGANG VON GOETHE ON WILHELM MEISTER'S FASCINATION WITH HAMLET

[Johann Wolfgang von Goethe (1749–1832), perhaps the greatest poet in German literature and author of *Faust* (1808–32), was an important figure in the Romantic movement in literature. In his novel, *Wilhelm Meister's Apprenticeship* (1795–96), Goethe depicts the young Wilhelm Meister becoming fascinated with the character of Hamlet, perhaps because he believes Hamlet to be similar in temperament to himself.]

Loving Shakespeare as our friend did, he failed not to lead round the conversation to the merits of that dramatist. Expressing, as he entertained, the liveliest hopes of the new epoch which these exquisite productions must form in Germany, he ere long introduced Hamlet, who had busied him so much of late.

Serlo declared that he would long ago have played the piece, had this been possible, and that he himself would willingly engage to act Polonius. He added, with a smile: "An Ophelia, too, will certainly turn up, if we had but a Prince."

Wilhelm did not notice that Aurelia seemed a little hurt at her brother's sarcasm. Our friend was in his proper vein, becoming copious and didactic, expounding how he would have Hamlet played. He circumstantially delivered to his hearers the opinions we before saw him busied with; taking all the trouble possible to make his notion of the matter acceptable, sceptical as Serlo showed himself regarding it. "Well, then," said the latter, finally, "suppose we grant you all this, what will you explain by it?"

"Much, everything," said Wilhelm. "Conceive a prince such as I have painted him, and that his father suddenly dies. Ambition and the love of rule are not the passions that inspire him. As a king's son he would have been contented; but now he is first constrained to consider the difference which separates a sovereign from a subject. The crown was not hereditary; yet a longer possession of it by his father would have strengthened the pretensions of an only son, and secured his hopes of the succession. In place of this, he now beholds himself excluded by his uncle, in spite of specious promises, most probably forever. He is now poor in goods and favour, and a stranger in the scene which from youth he had looked upon as his inheritance. His temper here assumes its first mournful tinge. He feels that now he is not more, that he is less, than a private nobleman; he offers himself as the servant of every one; he is not courteous and condescending, he is needy and degraded.

"His past condition he remembers as a vanished dream. It is in vain that his uncle strives to cheer him, to present his situation in another point of view. The feeling of his nothingness will not leave him.

"The second stroke that came upon him wounded deeper, bowed still more. It was the marriage of his mother. The faithful tender son had yet a mother, when his father passed away. He hoped, in the company of his surviving noble-minded parent, to reverence the heroic form of the departed; but his mother too he loses, and it is something worse than death that robs him of her. The trustful image, which a good child loves to form of its parents, is gone. With the dead there is no help; on the living no hold. She also is a woman, and her name is Frailty, like that of all her sex.

"Now first does he feel himself completely bent and orphaned; and no happiness of life can repay what he has lost. Not reflective or sorrowful by nature, reflection and sorrow have become for him a heavy obligation. It is thus that we see him first enter on the scene. I do not think that I have mixed aught foreign with the piece, or overcharged a single feature of it."

Serlo looked at his sister, and said, "Did I give thee a false picture of our friend? He begins well; he has still many things to tell us, many to persuade us of." Wilhelm asseverated loud-ly, that he meant not to persuade, but to convince; he begged for another moment's patience.

"Figure to yourselves this youth," cried he, "this son of princes; conceive him vividly, bring his state before your eyes, and then observe him when he learns that his father's spirit walks; stand by him in the terrors of the night, when the vener-able ghost itself appears before him. A horrid shudder passes over him; he speaks to the mysterious form; he sees it beckon him; he follows it, and hears. The fearful accusation of his uncle rings in his ears; the summons to revenge, and the piercing oft-repeated prayer, Remember me!

"And when the ghost has vanished, who is it that stands before us? A young hero panting for vengeance? A prince by birth, rejoicing to be called to punish the usurper of his crown? No! trouble and astonishment take hold of the solitary young man; he grows bitter against smiling villains, swears that he will not forget the spirit, and concludes with the significant ejaculation:

> The time is out of joint: O cursed spite,
> That ever I was born to set it right!

"In these words, I imagine, will be found the key to Hamlet's whole procedure. To me it is clear that Shakespeare meant, in the present case, to represent the effects of a great action laid upon a soul unfit for the performance of it. In this view the whole piece seems to me to be composed. There is an oak-tree planted in a costly jar, which should have borne only pleasant flowers in its bosom; the roots expand, the jar is shivered.

"A lovely, pure, noble and most moral nature, without the strength of nerve which forms a hero, sinks beneath a burden which it cannot bear and must not cast away. All duties are holy for him; the present is too hard. Impossibilities have been required of him; not in themselves impossibilities, but such for him. He winds, and turns, and torments himself; he advances and recoils; is ever put in mind, ever puts himself in mind; at last does all but lose his purpose from his thoughts; yet still without recovering his peace of mind."

—Johann Wolfgang von Goethe, *Willhelm Meister's Apprenticeship and Travels* (1795–96), tr. Thomas Carlyle (1824) (Boston: Houghton Mifflin, 1893), pp. 229–32

AUGUST WILHELM VON SCHLEGEL ON HAMLET'S FLAWS

[August Wilhelm von Schlegel (1767–1845) was a leading German critic who significantly influenced many English writers of the Romantic period. In his famous book, *Lectures on Dramatic Art and Literature* (1809), excerpted here, Schlegel disagrees with Goethe's praise of Hamlet, finding many flaws in his character.]

With respect to Hamlet's character: I cannot, as I understand the poet's views, pronounce altogether so favourable a sentence upon it as Goethe does. He is, it is true, of a highly cultivated mind, a prince of royal manners, endowed with the finest sense of propriety, susceptible of noble ambition, and open in the highest degree to an enthusiastic admiration of that excellence in others of which he himself is deficient. He acts the part of madness with unrivalled power, convincing the persons who are sent to examine into his supposed loss of reason, merely by telling them unwelcome truths, and rallying them with the most caustic wit. But in the resolutions which he so often embraces and always leaves unexecuted, his weakness is too apparent: he does himself only justice when he implies that there is no greater dissimilarity than between himself and Hercules. He is not solely impelled by necessity to artifice and dissimulation, he has a natural inclination for crooked ways; he is a hypocrite towards himself; his far-fetched scruples are often mere pretexts to cover his want of determination: thoughts, as he says on a different occasion, which have

> but one part wisdom
> And ever three parts coward.

He has been chiefly condemned both for his harshness in repulsing the love of Ophelia, which he himself had cherished, and for his insensibility at her death. But he is too much over-whelmed with his own sorrow to have any compassion to spare for others; besides his outward indifference gives us by no means the measure of his internal perturbation. On the other hand, we evidently perceive in him a malicious joy, when he has succeeded in getting rid of his enemies, more through necessity and accident, which alone are able to impel him to quick and decisive measures, than by the merit of his own courage, as he himself confesses after the murder of Polonius, and with respect to Rosencrantz and Guildenstern. Hamlet has no firm belief either in himself or in anything else: from expressions of religious confidence he passes over to sceptical doubts; he believes in the Ghost of his father as long as he sees it, but as soon as it has disappeared, it appears to him almost in the light of a deception. He has even gone so far as to say, "there is nothing either good or bad, but thinking makes it so;" with him the poet loses himself here in labyrinths of thought, in which neither end nor beginning is discoverable. The stars themselves, from the course of events, afford no answer to the question so urgently proposed to them. A voice from another world, commissioned it would appear, by heaven, demands vengeance for a monstrous enormity, and the demand remains without effect; the criminals are at least punished, but, as it were, by an accidental blow, and not in the solemn way requisite to convey to the world a warning example of justice; irresolute foresight, cunning treachery, and impetuous rage, hurry on to a common destruction; the less guilty and the innocent are equally involved in the general ruin. The destiny of humanity is there exhibited as a gigantic Sphinx, which threatens to precipitate into the abyss of scepticism all who are unable to solve her dreadful enigmas.

> —August Wilhelm von Schlegel, *Lectures on Dramatic Art and Literature* (1809), tr. John Black (1816), rev. A. S. W. Morrison (London: George Bell & Sons, 1894), pp. 405–6

SAMUEL TAYLOR COLERIDGE ON HAMLET'S INTELLECTUALISM

[Samuel Taylor Coleridge (1772–1834), aside from being one of the greatest British poets of the early nineteenth century, was also a penetrating critic. His most famous critical work is *Biographia Literaria* (1817). In 1819 he delivered a series of lectures on Shakespeare, which were published posthumously in his *Literary Remains* (1836–39). In this extract from that work, Coleridge studies Hamlet's psyche and finds that an excess of intellectualism and a lack of ability to act upon it is the crux of Hamlet's difficulties.]

The seeming inconsistencies in the conduct and character of Hamlet have long exercised the conjectural ingenuity of critics; and, as we are always loth to suppose that the cause of defective apprehension is in ourselves, the mystery has been too commonly explained by the very easy process of setting it down as in fact inexplicable, and by resolving the phenomenon into a misgrowth or *lusus* of the capricious and irregular genius of Shakspeare. The shallow and stupid arrogance of these vulgar and indolent decisions I would fain do my best to expose. I believe the character of Hamlet may be traced to Shakspeare's deep and accurate science in mental philosophy. Indeed, that this character must have some connection with the common fundamental laws of our nature may be assumed from the fact, that Hamlet has been the darling of every country in which the literature of England has been fostered. In order to understand him, it is essential that we should reflect on the constitution of our own minds. Man is distinguished from the brute animals in proportion as thought prevails over sense: but in the healthy processes of the mind, a balance is constantly maintained between the impressions from outward objects and the inward operations of the intellect;—for if there be an overbalance in the contemplative faculty, man thereby becomes the creature of mere meditation, and loses his natural power of action. Now one of Shakspeare's modes of creating characters is, to conceive any one intellectual or moral faculty in morbid excess, and then to place himself, Shakspeare, thus mutilated or diseased, under given circumstances. In Hamlet he seems to have wished to exemplify the moral necessity of a due balance between our attention to the objects of our senses, and our meditation on the workings of our minds,—an *equilibrium* between the real and the imaginary worlds. In Hamlet this balance is disturbed; his thoughts, and the images of his fancy, are far more vivid than his actual perceptions, and his very perceptions, instantly passing through the *medium* of his contemplations, acquire, as they pass, a form and a colour not naturally their own. Hence we see a great, an almost enormous, intellectual activity, and a proportionate aversion to real action consequent upon it, with all its symptoms and accompanying qualities. This character Shakspeare places in circumstances, under which it is obliged to act on the spur of the moment:— Hamlet is brave and careless of death; but he vacillates from sensibility, and procrastinates from thought, and loses the power of action in the energy of resolve. Thus it is that this tragedy presents a direct contrast to that of *Macbeth;* the one proceeds with the utmost slowness, the other with a crowded and breathless rapidity.

The effect of this overbalance of the imaginative power is beautifully illustrated in the everlasting broodings and superfluous activities of Hamlet's mind, which, unseated from its healthy relation, is constantly occupied with the world within, and abstracted from the world without,—giving substance to shadows, and throwing a mist over all common-place actualities. It is the nature of thought to be indefinite;—definiteness belongs to external imagery alone. Hence it is that the sense of sublimity arises, not from the sight of an outward object, but from the beholder's reflection upon it;—not from the sensuous impression, but from the imaginative reflex. Few have seen a celebrated waterfall without feeling something akin to disappointment: it is only subsequently that the image comes back full into the mind, and brings with it a train of grand or beautiful associations. Hamlet feels this; his senses are in a state of trance, and he looks upon external things as hieroglyphics. His soliloquy—

O! that this too too solid flesh would melt, &c.

springs from that craving after the indefinite—for that which is not—which most easily besets men of genius; and the self-delusion common to this temper of mind is finely exemplified in the character which Hamlet gives of himself:— ˌ

It cannot be
But I am pigeon-livered, and lack gall
To make oppression bitter.

He mistakes the seeing his chains for the breaking them, delays action till action is of no use, and dies the victim of mere circumstance and accident.

—Samuel Taylor Coleridge, "Hamlet" (1819), *Literary Remains,* ed. Henry Nelson Coleridge (London: William Pickering, 1836), Vol. 2, pp. 204–7

FRIEDRICH NIETZSCHE ON HAMLET AS THE DIONYSIAN MAN

[Friedrich Nietzsche (1844–1900) was one of the greatest philosophers of the nineteenth century, having written such works as *Thus Spake Zarathrustra* (1883–92) and *Beyond Good and Evil* (1886). His earliest work was *The Birth of Tragedy* (1872), in which he made his famous analysis of ancient Greek tragedy as embodying a combination of "Apollonian" (rational) and "Dionysiac" (emotional or passionate) qualities. In this extract from that work, Nietzsche sees Hamlet as exemplifying Dionysiac traits that lead to nausea and pessimism.]

For the rapture of the Dionysian state with its annihilation of the ordinary bounds and limits of existence contains, while it lasts, a *lethargic* element in which all personal experiences of the past become immersed. This chasm of oblivion separates the worlds of everyday reality and of Dionysian reality. But as soon as this everyday reality re-enters consciousness, it is experienced as such, with nausea: an ascetic, will-negating mood is the fruit of these states.

In this sense the Dionysian man resembles Hamlet: both have once looked truly into the essence of things, they have *gained knowledge,* and nausea inhibits action; for their action could not change anything in the eternal nature of things; they feel it to be ridiculous or humiliating that they should be asked to set right a world that is out of joint. Knowledge kills action; action requires the veils of illusion: that is the doctrine of Hamlet, not that cheap wisdom of Jack the Dreamer who reflects too much and, as it were, from an excess of possibilities does not get around to action. Not reflection, no—true knowledge, an insight into the horrible truth, outweighs any motive for action, both in Hamlet and in the Dionysian man.

—Friedrich Nietzsche, *The Birth of Tragedy* (1872), tr. Walter Kaufmann (New York: Vintage, 1967), pp. 59–60

OSCAR WILDE ON ROSENCRANTZ AND GUILDENSTERN

[Oscar Wilde (1854–1900), a leading British playwright, novelist, and poet, wrote several important works of criticism (especially "The Critic as Artist" [1891]) that helped to initiate the "art for art's sake" movement, in which art was shorn of moral or social obligations. In a long letter to his friend Lord Alfred Douglas, Wilde studies the characters of Rosencrantz and Guildenstern, seeing in their buffoonery a grim contrast to Hamlet's tragic awareness.]

I know of nothing in all Drama more incomparable from the point of view of Art, or more suggestive in its subtlety of observation, than Shakespeare's drawing of Rosencrantz and Guildenstern. They are Hamlet's college friends. They have been his companions. They bring with them memories of pleasant days together. At the moment when they come across him in the play he is staggering under the weight of a burden intolerable to one of his temperament. The dead have come armed out of the grave to impose on him a mission at once too great and too mean for him. He is a dreamer, and he is called upon to act. He has the nature of the poet and he is asked to grapple with the common complexities of cause and effect, with life in its practical realisation, of which he knows nothing, not with life in its ideal essence, of which he knows much. He has no conception of what to do, and his folly is to feign folly. Brutus used madness as a cloak to conceal the sword of his purpose, the dagger of his will, but to Hamlet madness is a mere mask for the hiding of weakness. In the making of mows and jests he sees a chance of delay. He keeps playing with action, as an artist plays with a theory. He makes himself the spy of his proper actions, and listening to his own words knows them to be but "words, words, words." Instead of trying to be the hero of his own history, he seeks to be the spectator of his own tragedy. He disbelieves in everything, including himself, and yet his doubt helps him not, as it comes not from scepticism but from a divided will.

Of all this, Guildenstern and Rosencrantz realise nothing. They bow and smirk and smile, and what the one says the other echoes with sicklier iteration. When at last, by means of the play within the play and the puppets in their dalliance, Hamlet "catches the conscience" of the King, and drives the wretched man in terror from his throne, Guildenstern and Rosencrantz see no more in his conduct than a rather painful breach of court-etiquette. That is as far as they can attain to in "the contemplation of the spectacle of life with appropriate emotions." They are close to his very secret and know nothing of it. Nor would there be any use in telling them. They are the little cups that can hold so much and no more. Towards the close it is suggested that, caught in a cunning springe set for another, they have met, or may meet with a violent and sudden death. But a tragic ending of this kind, though touched by Hamlet's humour with something of the surprise and justice of comedy, is really not for such as they. They never die. Horatio who, in order to "report Hamlet and his cause aright to the unsatisfied,"

> Absents him from felicity a while
> And in this harsh world draws his breath in pain,

dies, though not before an audience, and leaves no brother. But Guildenstern and Rosencrantz are as immortal as Angelo and Tartuffe, and should rank with them. They are what modern life has contributed to the antique ideal of friendship. He who writes a new *De Amicitia* must find a niche for them and praise them in Tusculan prose. They are types fixed for all time. To censure them would show a lack of appreciation. They are merely out of their sphere: that is all. In sublimity of soul there is no contagion. High thoughts and high emotions are by their very existence isolated. What Ophelia herself could not understand was not to be realised by "Guildenstern and gentle Rosencrantz," by "Rosencrantz and gentle Guildenstern."
—Oscar Wilde, Letter to Lord Alfred Douglass (January–March 1897), *Selected Letters of Oscar Wilde,* ed. Rupert Hart-Davis (Oxford: Oxford University Press, 1979), pp. 232–33

SIGMUND FREUD ON HAMLET AND HIS FATHER

[Sigmund Freud (1856–1939) is the German psychologist who founded psychoanalysis. Among his most important books are *The Interpretation of Dreams* (German edition 1900; English translation 1913) and *A*

General Introduction to Psychoanalysis (German edition 1916–17; English translation 1920). Freud frequently devoted his attention to the study of literature from a psychoanalytic perspective. In this extract from *The Interpretation of Dreams,* Freud sees Hamlet's irresoluteness as reflecting his mixed feelings about his father.]

Another of the great creations of tragic poetry, Shakespeare's *Hamlet,* has its roots in the same soil as *Oedipus Rex.* But the changed treatment of the same material reveals the whole difference in the mental life of these two widely separated epochs of civilization: the secular advance of repression in the emotional life of mankind. In the *Oedipus* the child's wishful phantasy that underlies it is brought into the open and realized as it would be in a dream. In *Hamlet* it remains repressed; and—just as in the case of a neurosis—we only learn of its existence from its inhibiting consequences. Strangely enough, the overwhelming effect produced by the more modern tragedy has turned out to be compatible with the fact that people have remained completely in the dark as to the hero's character. The play is built up on Hamlet's hesitations over fulfilling the task of revenge that is assigned to him; but its text offers no reasons or motives for these hesitations and an immense variety of attempts at interpreting them have failed to produce a result. According to the view which was originated by Goethe and is still the prevailing one to-day, Hamlet represents the type of man whose power of direct action is paralysed by an excessive development of his intellect. (He is 'sicklied o'er with the pale cast of thought'.) According to another view, the dramatist has tried to portray a pathologically irresolute character which might be classed as neurasthenic. The plot of the drama shows us, however, that Hamlet is far from being represented as a person incapable of taking any action. We see him doing so on two occasions: first in a sudden outburst of temper, when he runs his sword through the eavesdropper behind the arras, and secondly in a premeditated and even crafty fashion, when, with all the callousness of a Renaissance prince, he sends the two courtiers to the death that had been planned for himself. What is it, then, that inhibits him in fulfilling the task set him by his father's ghost? The answer, once again, is that it is the peculiar nature of the task. Hamlet is able to do anything—except take vengeance on the man who did away with his father and took that father's place with his mother, the man who shows him the repressed wishes of his own childhood realized. Thus the loathing which should drive him on to revenge is replaced in him by self-reproaches, by scruples of conscience, which remind him that he himself is literally no better than the sinner whom he is to punish. Here I have translated into conscious terms what was bound to remain unconscious in Hamlet's mind; and if anyone is inclined to call him a hysteric, I can only accept the fact as one is implied by my interpretation. The distaste for sexuality expressed by Hamlet in his conversation with Ophelia fits in very well with this: the same distaste which was destined to take possession of the poet's mind more and more during the years that followed, and which reached its extreme expression in *Timon of Athens*. For it can of course only be the poet's own mind which confronts us in Hamlet. I observe in a book on Shakespeare by Georg Brandes (1896) a statement that *Hamlet* was written immediately after the death of Shakespeare's father (in 1601), that is, under the immediate impact of his bereavement and, as we may well assume, while his childhood feelings about his father had been freshly revived. It is known, too, that Shakespeare's own son who died at an early age bore the name of 'Hamnet', which is identical with 'Hamlet'. Just as *Hamlet* deals with the relation of a son to his parents, so *Macbeth* (written at approximately the same period) is concerned with the subject of childlessness. But just as all neurotic symptoms, and, for that matter, dreams, are capable of being 'over-interpreted' and indeed need to be, if they are to be fully understood, so all genuinely creative writings are the product of more than a single motive and more than a single impulse in the poet's mind, and are open to more than a single interpretation. In what I have written I have only attempted to interpret the deepest layer of impulses in the mind of the creative writer.

—Sigmund Freud, *The Interpretation of Dreams* (1900), tr. James Strachey et al. (London: Hogarth Press/Institute of Psychoanalysis, 1953), pp. 264–66

A. C. BRADLEY ON QUEEN GERTRUDE

[A. C. Bradley (1851–1935) was the leading British Shakespeare scholar of his time. He taught at the University of Liverpool, the University of Glasgow, and at Oxford University, and wrote *Oxford Lectures on Poetry* (1909) and *A Miscellany* (1929). In this extract, taken from his celebrated book, *Shakespearean Tragedy* (1904), Bradley finds that Shakespeare has drawn the character of Gertrude with a unique mixture of the grotesque and the pathetic.]

The answers to two questions asked about the Queen are, it seems to me, practically certain. (1) She did not merely marry a second time with indecent haste; she was false to her husband while he lived. This is surely the most natural interpretation of the words of the Ghost (I. v. 41f.), coming, as they do, before his account of the murder. And against this testimony what force has the objection that the queen in the *Murder of Gonzago* is not represented as an adulteress? Hamlet's mark in arranging the play-scene was not his mother, whom besides he had been expressly ordered to spare (I. v. 84f.).

(2) On the other hand, she was *not* privy to the murder of her husband, either before the deed or after it. There is no sign of her being so, and there are clear signs that she was not. The representation of the murder in the play-scene does not move her; and when her husband starts from his throne, she innocently asks him, 'How fares my lord?' In the interview with Hamlet, when her son says of his slaughter of Polonius,

'A bloody deed!' Almost as bad, good mother,
As kill a king and marry with his brother,

the astonishment of her repetition 'As kill a king!' is evidently genuine; and, if it had not been so, she would never have had the hardihood to exclaim:

What have I done, that thou darest wag thy tongue
In noise so rude against me?

Further, it is most significant that when she and the King speak together alone, nothing that is said by her or to her implies her knowledge of the secret.

The Queen was not a bad-hearted woman, not at all the woman to think little of murder. But she had a soft animal nature, and was very dull and very shallow. She loved to be happy, like a sheep in the sun; and, to do her justice, it pleased her to see others happy, like more sheep in the sun. She never saw that drunkenness is disgusting till Hamlet told her so; and, though she knew that he considered her marriage 'o'er-hasty' (II. ii. 57), she was untroubled by any shame at the feelings which had led to it. It was pleasant to sit upon her throne and see smiling faces round her, and foolish and unkind in Hamlet to persist in grieving for his father instead of marrying Ophelia and making everything comfortable. She was fond of Ophelia and genuinely attached to her son (though willing to see her lover exclude him from the throne); and, no doubt, she considered equality of rank a mere trifle compared with the claims of love. The belief at the bottom of her heart was that the world is a place constructed simply that people may be happy in it in a good-humoured sensual fashion.

Her only chance was to be made unhappy. When affliction comes to her, the good in her nature struggles to the surface through the heavy mass of sloth. Like other faulty characters in Shakespeare's tragedies, she dies a better woman than she had lived. When Hamlet shows her what she has done she feels genuine remorse. It is true, Hamlet fears it will not last, and so at the end of the interview (III. iv. 180ff.) he adds a warning that, if she betrays him, she will ruin herself as well. It is true too that there is no sign of her obeying Hamlet in breaking off her most intimate connection with the King. Still she does feel remorse; and she loves her son, and does not betray him. She gives her husband a false account of Polonius's death, and is silent about the appearance of the Ghost. She becomes miserable;

> To her sick soul, as sin's true nature is,
> Each toy seems prologue to some great amiss.

She shows spirit when Laertes raises the mob, and one respects her for standing up for her husband when she can do nothing to help her son. If she had sense to realise Hamlet's purpose, or the probability of the King's taking some desperate step to foil it, she must have suffered torture in those days. But perhaps she was too dull.

The last we see of her, at the fencing-match, is most characteristic. She is perfectly serene. Things have slipped back into their groove, and she has no apprehensions. She is, however, disturbed and full of sympathy for her son, who is out of condition and pants and perspires. These are afflictions she can thoroughly feel for, though they are even more common than the death of a father. But then she meets her death because she cannot resist the wish to please her son by drinking to his success. And more: when she falls dying, and the King tries to make out that she is merely swooning at the sight of blood, she collects her energies to deny it and to warn Hamlet:

> No, no, the drink, the drink,—O my dear Hamlet,—
> The drink, the drink! I am poison'd.   [*Dies.*

Was ever any other writer at once so pitiless and so just as Shakespeare? Did ever any other mingle the grotesque and the pathetic with a realism so daring and yet so true to 'the modesty of nature'?
>—A. C. Bradley, *Shakespearean Tragedy* (London: Macmillan, 1904), pp. 166–68

T. S. Eliot on *Hamlet* as a Failure

[T. S. Eliot (1888–1965), although born in St. Louis, spent most of his adult life in England and regarded himself as an English writer. Aside from being one of the leading poets of the early twentieth century (*The Waste Land*, 1922; *Four Quartets*, 1935–42), Eliot was an influential critic and essayist. In the following early essay on *Hamlet,* Eliot presents his celebrated view that the play is a failure because Hamlet's emotions are in excess of the facts on which they are based.]

The only way of expressing emotion in the form of art is by finding an "objective correlative"; in other words, a set of objects, a situation, a chain of events which shall be the formula of that *particular* emotion; such that when the external facts, which must terminate in sensory experience, are given, the emotion is immediately evoked. If you examine any of Shakespeare's more successful tragedies, you will find this exact equivalence; you will find that the state of mind of Lady Macbeth walking in her sleep has been communicated to you by a skilful accumulation of imagined sensory impressions; the words of Macbeth on hearing of his wife's death strike us as if, given the sequence of events, these words were automatically released by the last event in the series. The artistic "inevitability" lies in this complete adequacy of the external to the emotion; and this is precisely what is deficient in *Hamlet.* Hamlet (the man) is dominated by an emotion which is inexpressible, because it is in *excess* of the facts as they appear. And the supposed identity of Hamlet with his author is genuine to this point: that Hamlet's bafflement at the absence of objective equivalent to his feelings is a prolongation of the bafflement of his creator in the face of his artistic problem. Hamlet is up against the difficulty that his disgust is occasioned by his mother, but that his mother is not an adequate equivalent for it; his disgust envelopes and exceeds her. It is thus a feeling which he cannot understand; he cannot objectify it, and it therefore remains to poison life and obstruct action. None of the possible actions can satisfy it; and nothing that Shakespeare can do with the plot can express Hamlet for him. And it must be noticed that the very nature of the *données* of the problem precludes objective equivalence. To have heightened the criminality of Gertrude would have been to provide the formula for a totally different emotion in Hamlet; it is just *because* her character is so negative and insignificant that she arouses in Hamlet the feeling which she is incapable of representing.

The "madness" of Hamlet lay to Shakespeare's hand; in the earlier play a simple ruse, and to the end, we may presume, understood as a ruse by the audience. For Shakespeare it is less than madness and more than feigned. The levity of Hamlet, his repetition of phrase, his puns, are not part of a deliberate plan of dissimulation, but a form of emotional relief. In the character Hamlet it is the buffoonery of an emotion which can find no outlet in action; in the dramatist it is the buffoonery of an emotion which he cannot express in art. The intense feeling, ecstatic or terrible, without an object or exceeding its object, is something which every person of sensibility has known; it is doubtless a subject of study for pathologists. It often occurs in adolescence: the ordinary person puts these feelings to sleep, or trims down his feelings to fit the business world; the artist keeps them alive by his ability to intensify the world to his emotions. The Hamlet of Laforgue is an adolescent; the Hamlet of Shakespeare is not, he has not that explanation and excuse. We must simply admit that here Shakespeare tackled a problem which proved too much for him. Why he attempted it at all is an insoluble puzzle; under compulsion of what experience he attempted to express the inexpressibly horrible, we cannot ever know. We need a great many facts in his biography; and we should like to know whether, and when, and after or at the same time as what personal experience, he read Montaigne, II. xii, "Apologie de Raimond Sebond." We should have, finally, to know something which is by hypothesis unknowable, for we assume it to be an experience which, in the manner indicated, exceeded the facts. We should have to understand things which Shakespeare did not understand himself.

 —T. S. Eliot, "Hamlet" (1919), *Selected Essays* (New York: Harcourt, Brace & World, 1950), pp. 124–26

C. S. LEWIS ON HAMLET'S SOLILOQUIES

[C. S. Lewis (1898–1963), although currently best known today for his "Chronicles of Narnia," a series of children's books, was a prolific novelist, scholar, and critic. In the following extract, Lewis maintains that

Hamlet's richly philosophical soliloquies are designed
not so much to reveal Hamlet's own character as to
utter broad truths about humanity.]

For what, after all, is happening to us when we read any of
Hamlet's great speeches? We see visions of the flesh dissolving
into a dew, of the world like an unweeded garden. We think of
memory reeling in its 'distracted globe'. We watch him scam-
pering hither and thither like a maniac to avoid the voices
wherewith he is haunted. Someone says 'Walk out of the air',
and we hear the words 'Into my grave' spontaneously respond
to it. We think of being bounded in a nut-shell and king of infi-
nite space: but for bad dreams. There's the trouble, for 'I am
most dreadfully attended'. We see the picture of a dull and
muddy-mettled rascal, a John-a-dreams, somehow unable to
move while ultimate dishonour is done him. We listen to his
fear lest the whole thing may be an illusion due to melancholy.
We get the sense of sweet relief at the words 'shuffled off this
mortal coil' but mixed with the bottomless doubt about what
may follow then. We think of bones and skulls, of women
breeding sinners, and of how some, to whom all this experience is a sealed book, can yet dare death and danger 'for an
eggshell'. But do we really enjoy these things, do we go back
to them, because they show us Hamlet's character? Are they,
from *that* point of view, so very interesting? Does the mere fact
that a young man, literally haunted, dispossessed, and lacking
friends, should feel thus, tell us anything remarkable? Let me
put my question in another way. If instead of the speeches he
actually utters about the firmament and man in his scene with
Rosencrantz and Guildenstern Hamlet had merely said, 'I don't
seem to enjoy things the way I used to,' and talked in that
fashion throughout, should we find him interesting? I think the
answer is 'Not very.' It may be replied that if he talked com-
monplace prose he would reveal his character less vividly. I am
not so sure. He would certainly have revealed *something* less
vividly; but would that something be himself? It seems to me
that 'this majestical roof' and 'What a piece of work is a man'
give me primarily an impression not of the sort of person he
must be to lose the estimation of things but of the things themselves and their great value; and that I should be able to dis-
cern, though with very faint interest, the same condition of loss

in a personage who was quite unable so to put before me what he was losing. And I do not think it true to reply that he would be a different character if he spoke less poetically. This point is often misunderstood. We sometimes speak as if the characters in whose mouths Shakespeare puts great poetry were poets: in the sense that Shakespeare was depicting men of poetical genius. But surely this is like thinking that Wagner's Wotan is the dramatic portrait of a baritone? In opera song is the medium by which the representation is made and not part of the thing represented. The actors sing; the dramatic personages are feigned to be speaking. The only character who sings dramatically in *Figaro* is Cherubino. Similarly in poetical drama poetry is the medium, not part of the delineated characters. While the actors speak poetry written for them by the poet, the dramatic personages are supposed to be merely talking. If ever there is occasion to *represent* poetry (as in the play scene from *Hamlet*), it is put into a different metre and strongly stylized so as to prevent confusion.

I trust that my conception is now becoming clear. I believe that we read Hamlet's speeches with interest chiefly because they describe so well a certain spiritual region through which most of us have passed and anyone in his circumstances might be expected to pass, rather than because of our concern to understand how and why this particular man entered it. I foresee an objection on the ground that I am thus really admitting his 'character' in the only sense that matters and that all characters whatever could be equally well talked away by the method I have adopted. But I do really find a distinction. When I read about Mrs Proudie I am not in the least interested in seeing the world from her point of view, for her point of view is not interesting; what does interest me is precisely the sort of person she was. In *Middlemarch* no reader wants to see Casaubon through Dorothea's eyes; the pathos, the comedy, the value of the whole thing is to understand Dorothea and see how such an illusion was inevitable for her. In Shakespeare himself I find Beatrice to be a character who could not be thus dissolved. We are interested not in some vision seen through her eyes, but precisely in the wonder of her being the girl she is. A comparison of the sayings we remember from her part with those we remember from Hamlet's brings out the contrast. On the one hand, 'I wonder that you will still be talking, Signior Benedick', 'There was a star danced and under that I was born', 'Kill Claudio'; on the other, 'The undiscovered country, from whose bourne no traveller returns', 'Use every man after his desert, and who should 'scape whipping?', 'The rest is silence.' Particularly noticeable is the passage where Hamlet professes to be describing his own character. 'I am myself indifferent honest, but yet I could accuse me of such things that it were better my mother had not borne me: I am very proud, revengeful, ambitious'. It is, of course, possible to devise some theory which explains these self-accusations in terms of character. But long before we have done so the real significance of the lines has taken possession of our imagination for ever. 'Such fellows as I' does not mean 'such fellows as Goethe's Hamlet, or Coleridge's Hamlet, or any Hamlet': it means *men*—creatures shapen in sin and conceived in iniquity—and the vast, empty visions of them 'crawling between earth and heaven' is what really counts and really carries the burden of the play.

—C. S. Lewis, "Hamlet: The Prince or the Poem?" (1942), *Selected Literary Essays*, ed. Walter Hooper (Cambridge: Cambridge University Press, 1969), pp. 100–102

HAROLD C. GODDARD ON THE ROLE OF *HAMLET* IN SHAKESPEARE'S DEVELOPMENT

[Harold C. Goddard (1878–1950) was for many years head of the English department at Swarthmore College. He was the author of *Studies in New England Transcendentalism* (1906) and the editor of an edition of Ralph Waldo Emerson's essays (1926). In this extract, taken from his important book, *The Meaning of Shakespeare* (1951), Goddard examines *Hamlet* in the context of Shakespeare's entire work and finds it a significant step in the development of Shakespeare's conception of character.]

"But in that case why didn't Shakespeare make his intention clear?" A question that implies a profound misapprehension of the nature of poetic, if not of dramatic, art.

Of course Shakespeare expected his audience to assume that Hamlet should kill the King, exactly as he expected them to assume that Katherine was a shrew, and that Henry V was a glorious hero for attempting to steal the kingdom of France. He was not so ignorant of human nature as not to know how it reacts under the stimulus of primitive emotion. He understood too that what ought to be can be seen only against a background of what is. Carlyle spoke of the Paolo and Francesca incident in *The Inferno* as a thing woven of rainbows on a background of eternal black. And Hamlet himself declared:

> I'll be your foil, Laertes; in mine ignorance
> Your skill shall, like a star i' the darkest night,
> Stick fiery off indeed.

The contrast need not always be so extreme. The setting is more ordinarily terrestrial and diurnal than infernal, or even nocturnal. If, enthralled by its familiarity, we do not alter the focus of our eyes to see what may be unfamiliar and perhaps nearly invisible in the foreground, how is that the poet's fault? This is not his lookout. His business is to create a work of art. How it is taken is not his responsibility. "Here it is," he seems to say, as perhaps God did when he made the world, "take it, and see what you can make of it." And different men make very different things. To all of us in life appearances are deceitful. To all save the wisest characters in a work of dramatic art, if it be true to life, they should be even more so. The spectator or reader of that work takes delight in their delusions. But meanwhile from a higher level the poet may be deluding him. Living would lose all its challenge if everything were made so plain that anybody could understand it all the first time. And so would reading. You plunge into a poem as you plunge into battle—at your peril. "That which can be made explicit to the idiot," said Blake, "is not worth my care."

This procedure is not trickery. Even the alertest reader must be partly taken in the first time or he will miss more than he gains. A book that can be comprehended at a first reading is not imaginative literature. Dostoevsky's novels, for instance, contain many dreams and hallucinations which the reader is intended to mistake for occurrences in the objective world until, later, he realizes that the person having the experience was asleep or in a trance. That is as it should be. For dreams are true while they last, and Dostoevsky's technique leads us to identify ourselves with the dreamer. A too critical reader who sees through the device deprives himself of the very experience he would understand. Intellectuals cannot read. A child lost in a story is the model of right first reading. The more ingenuous we are the first time the better. But not the second and third times. Then the critical intellect should begin to check the imagination—or check on it rather. Shakespeare, I am convinced, wanted us at first to believe that Hamlet ought to kill the King in order that we might undergo his agony with him. But he did not want us, I am equally convinced, to persist in that belief. We must view Hamlet first under the aspect of time so that later we may view him under the aspect of eternity. We must be him before we can understand him.

And here, oddly, we have an advantage over Shakespeare. The author of *Hamlet,* when he wrote it, had not had the privilege of reading *King Lear* and other post-Hamletian masterpieces. But we have had it, and can read *Hamlet* in their light. This does not mean that we import into *Hamlet* from later plays anything that is not already there. A work of art must stand or fall by itself. It merely means that, with vision sharpened by later plays, we are enabled to see in *Hamlet* what was already there but hidden from us—as a later dream does not alter an earlier one but may render it intelligible because of a mutual relation. In some sense or other, as we have seen, Hamlet's problem must have been Shakespeare's. He doubtless wrote the play in part to make that problem clear, just as Tolstoy, to make his problem clear, wrote *Anna Karenina. Hamlet* being only a step in its solution, its author could not conceivably have caught its full import at once. But we can see, as later he could see, whither it was tending, as a prophecy is remembered and illuminated when it is fulfilled. However much above us Shakespeare may be in genius, at any particular moment in his development we are beyond him in time. To that extent we are on the mountain while he is on the road.

And even if we do not look beyond *Hamlet,* our vantage point enables us to see from the past the direction that road was taking. Roads, to be sure, may make unexpected turns, and even a long-maintained general course is no guarantee against its interruption. But highways of Shakespearean breadth seldom go off abruptly at right angles. And so it is permissible to ask as we come to *Hamlet:* What, judging from what he had been doing, might Shakespeare be expected to do next?

The answer is plain. Having given us in Hal-Henry (not to mention Romeo and Richard II) a divided man easily won by circumstances to the side of violence, and in Brutus a man so won only after a brief but terrible inner struggle, what then? Why, naturally, the next step in the progression: a divided man won to the side of violence only after a protracted struggle. And this is precisely what we have in Hamlet. Moreover, there is a passage in the play that confirms just this development. Indeed, as the word "development" suggests, a better metaphor than the road is the figure of an unfolding organism.
—Harold C. Goddard, *The Meaning of Shakespeare* (Chicago: University of Chicago Press, 1951), pp. 336–38

TERENCE EAGLETON ON HAMLET AND HIS SOCIETY

[Terence Eagleton (b. 1943) is a distinguished British literary critic who has specialized in the analysis of literature from a sociopolitical perspective of a sort often associated with Marxist criticism. Among his many books are *Criticism and Ideology* (1976), *Literary Theory: An Introduction* (1983), and *William Shakespeare* (1986). In this extract from his 1967 book on Shakespeare, Eagleton believes Hamlet's vacillation stems from his inability to find "authenticity" either within or outside of his society.]

Society denies Hamlet authenticity: it asks him to surrender up his own desires, his love for Ophelia and his reluctance to be limited by a fixed role, and take on an official function. Life on these terms, on the terms of Osric and Rosencrantz and Guildenstern, is clearly unacceptable for Hamlet: he is intent on not being a puppet. But Hamlet's insistence on not being a puppet leads, finally, to a delight in resisting any kind of defini-tion: it becomes, in fact, socially irresponsible, a merely nega-tive response. This is the really tragic tension in the play, the central dilemma. The significant actions which are available to Hamlet as formal modes of self-definition, the actions of killing Claudius and behaving as prince, are not the actions in which he can find himself authentically; therefore he is unable to act. But the real tragedy of a man who is unable to find self-defini-tion within formal social patterns, who can preserve his sense of identity only in opposition to these patterns, is that this identity then becomes unreal, negative. A self which can know itself only in constant opposition to its context finally destroys itself. This is the savage irony of the authentic man in a false society, the irony, to some degree, of Achilles in *Troilus;* the man who can find himself only outside his society's terms will disintegrate because of his very lack of that offered social verifi-cation of his existence which he is rejecting as false. Society may indeed be seen as false, its offered definitions as distort-ing, but it is still the only available way for a man to confirm himself as real, to objectify and know himself in public action. A man who does not objectify himself in action becomes un-real, as Achilles, according to Ulysses, is unreal; he loses, too, that spontaneity and truth-to-self which is the very ground of his opposition to the society.

This is Hamlet's situation. Hamlet must refuse to act in the public ways open to him because they seem to him false defi-nitions of himself; but his refusal to act means that he begins to lose hold on his identity, to lose spontaneous life. He turns from the public roles and actions to the personal relationship with Ophelia, looking there for a kind of definition, to find that this too has been absorbed into the public pattern: Ophelia has made an inauthentic choice, like Rosencrantz and Guildenstern, she has wavered between Polonius and Hamlet and chosen the former. Hamlet, now, cannot even find the authentic self-expression he is looking for in the margins of society: he is stirred into spontaneous life only momentarily, with Horatio or the actors. He can now preserve his integrity only by evading the offered definitions, and this involves a state of constant fluidity: to be himself he must keep himself free from the limiting demands of society, he must keep one jump ahead all the time. But the effort of doing this, paradoxically, is destructive of the very integrity he hopes to preserve; he, like the court, becomes involved in secretive and calculating politics, only in his case the politics, ironically, is a way of staying free from the machinations of the others. In a false society, there are a number of ways of preserving integrity, but they are all self-defeating. A man, to avoid the exploitation of others, may make himself opaque, refuse self-disclosure in action, as Hamlet does; but to refuse action is to stagnate, to lose spontaneity. He may, on the other hand, try to play the society's game of manipulation, and by playing it better than they do hoist them with their own petard; again, this involves a surrender of integrity, a sharing in the shifty tactics of others. Hamlet does this, and becomes like Claudius:

> HAMLET: 'Tis dangerous when the baser nature comes
> Between the pass and fell incensed points
> Of mighty opposites.
> HORATIO: Why, what a king is this! (V, 2)

Hamlet is completely trapped: he can find authenticity neither within nor outside society, since both to step outside the official nexus of the court, and to commit himself to it, involves loss of integrity, disintegration.

—Terence Eagleton, *Shakespeare and Society: Critical Studies in Shakespearean Drama* (New York: Schocken Books, 1967), pp. 61–63

RENÉ GIRARD ON *HAMLET* AS A REVENGE TRAGEDY

[René Girard (b. 1923), Andrew P. Hammond Professor of French at Stanford University, is the author of many important works of criticism and critical theory, including *Deceit, Desire, and the Novel* (1977), *Violence and the Sacred* (1977), and *A Theater of Envy: William Shakespeare* (1991). In this extract, Girard studies *Hamlet* in the context of the popular Elizabethan tradition of the revenge tragedy.]

Hamlet belongs to the genre of the revenge tragedy, as hackneyed and yet inescapable in Shakespeare's days as the "thriller" in ours to a television writer. In *Hamlet* Shakespeare turned this necessity for a playwright to go on writing the same old revenge tragedies into an opportunity to debate almost openly for the first time the questions I have tried to define. The weariness with revenge and *katharsis* which can be read, I believe, in the margins of the earlier plays must really exist because, in *Hamlet,* it moves to the center of the stage and becomes fully articulated.

Some writers who were not necessarily the most unimaginative found it difficult, we are told, to postpone for the whole duration of the lengthy Elizabethan play an action that had never been in doubt in the first place and that is always the same anyway. Shakespeare can turn this tedious chore into the most brilliant feat of theatrical *double entendre* because the tedium of revenge is really what he wants to talk about, and he wants to talk about it in the usual Shakespearean fashion; he will denounce the revenge theater and all its works with the utmost daring without denying his mass audience the *katharsis* it demands, without depriving himself of the dramatic success that is necessary to his own career as a dramatist.

If we assume that Shakespeare really had this double goal in mind, we will find that some unexplained details in the play become intelligible and that the function of many obscure scenes becomes obvious.

In order to perform revenge with conviction, you must believe in the justice of your own cause. The revenge seeker will not believe in his own cause unless he believes in the guilt of his intended victim. And the guilt of that intended victim entails in turn the innocence of that victim's victim. If the victim's victim is already a killer and if the revenge seeker reflects a little too much on the circularity of revenge, his faith in vengeance must collapse.

This is exactly what we have in *Hamlet*. It cannot be without a purpose that Shakespeare suggests the old Hamlet, the murdered king, was a murderer himself. In the various sources of the play there may be indications to that effect, but Shakespeare would have omitted them if he had wanted to strengthen the case for revenge. However nasty Claudius may look, he cannot look nasty enough if he appears in a context of previous revenge; he cannot generate, as a villain, the absolute passion and dedication demanded of Hamlet. The problem with Hamlet is that he cannot forget the context. As a result, the crime by Claudius looks to him like one more link in an already long chain, and his own revenge will look like still another link, perfectly identical to all the other links.

In a world where every ghost, dead or alive, can only perform the same action, revenge, or clamor for more of the same from beyond the grave, all voices are interchangeable. You can never know with certainty which ghost is addressing whom. It is one and the same thing for Hamlet to question his own identity and to question the ghost's identity, and his authority.

To seek singularity in revenge is a vain enterprise, but to shrink from revenge in a world that looks upon it as a "sacred duty" is to exclude oneself from society, to become a nonentity once more. There is no way out for Hamlet and he shifts endlessly from one impasse to the other, unable to make up his mind because neither choice makes sense.

If all characters are caught in a cycle of revenge that extends in all directions beyond the limits of its action, *Hamlet* has no beginning and no end. The play collapses. The trouble with the hero is that he does not believe in his play half as much as the critics do. He understands revenge and the theater too well to assume willingly a role chosen for him by others. His sentiments are those, in other words, which we have surmised in Shakespeare himself. What the hero feels in regard to the act of revenge, the creator feels in regard to revenge as theater.

The public wants vicarious victims and the playwright must oblige. Tragedy is revenge. Shakespeare is tired of revenge, and yet he cannot give it up, or he gives up his audience and his identity as a playwright. Shakespeare turns a typical revenge topic, *Hamlet*, into a meditation on his predicament as a playwright.

—René Girard, "Hamlet's Dull Revenge" (1984), *Literary Theory/Renaissance Texts*, ed. Patricia Parker and David Quint (Baltimore: Johns Hopkins University Press, 1986), pp. 282–84

JOSEPH H. SUMMERS ON THE MORALITY OF MURDER IN *HAMLET*

[Joseph H. Summers (b. 1920) is former professor of English at the University of Rochester and a leading scholar on seventeenth-century literature. Among his books are *George Herbert: His Religion and Art* (1954) and *The Heirs of Donne and Jonson* (1970). In this extract, taken from his 1984 book on Shakespeare, Summers maintains that in the context of its times, *Hamlet* portrays the act of murder to avenge dishonor as both a proper action and as a defiance of Christian notions of forgiveness.]

Within medieval and Renaissance societies, the duty to avenge familial murders and acts of dishonour was frequently in direct conflict with the Christian imperative to forgive one's enemies and with the civic laws against private vengeance. In most Renaissance plays, assumption of the revenger's role almost inevitably resulted in the moral debasement and physical destruction of the avenger in the process of accomplishing his revenge. Anne Barton has remarked that within the theatre we ordinarily begin to feel alienated from the revenger the moment he decides to kill:

> Only in Shakespeare's *Hamlet* does the audience retain sympathy for the hero from beginning to end. This is no mean dramaturgical feat, considering that Hamlet is responsible, either directly or indirectly, for the death of at least five other characters in the tragedy before he finally kills Claudius.

One of the means by which the play accomplishes that feat is by presenting the major conflict within Hamlet's mind and soul as a conflict between a view of human life and the universe as admirable and even blessed ('this goodly frame the earth. . . . What piece of work is a man'—II. ii. 298–303), and a view of an individual supernaturally devoted to the single-minded and private pursuit and murder of an uncle, a stepfather, and a king. It is, we recognize, literally impossible for anyone to retain the former view and choose to act in the latter fashion. If a hero attempts to do so, he will suffer astonishingly: he will likely come to view the world as corrupt and diseased rather than 'goodly'; he may experience moral and sexual nausea; he may come near to madness; and he may wish, momentarily at least, to die.

However, the primary reason that Hamlet cannot come to firm and continuous resolution to undertake the murder of Claudius probably has less to do with moral or psychological issues than with dramatic ones—it may be less a problem for Hamlet (or for Shakespeare) than for the audience. It is we who cannot bear that such a golden figure, an ideal prince supremely gifted, should kill in cold blood. The conventions, both dramatic and fictional, may be morally questionable, but they are relatively clear. We can contemplate the moral decline, decay, and death of a relatively flawed figure with interest and even fascination. Thus the limited and relatively unintelligent Laertes simple-mindedly becomes the tool of Claudius, and, abandoning all values except those of revenge and betraying his own honour in the name of honour, dies by his own dishonourable weapons; and we, along with Hamlet, can forgive him when he repents, confesses, and asks pardon. We will watch with horror the spiritual suicide and eventual death of a heroic figure like Macbeth who, consumed by ambition, knowingly makes a pact with evil. We can acknowledge the fact that inflexible heroic figures like Coriolanus or even Lear will almost inevitably be destroyed by the changing demands of the world and their own ignorance and failures in sympathy or love; we will watch the process with compelling interest as well as pain. We can accept, however regretfully, the fact that even ideal, golden heroes do not always win, but may be defeated and killed by the forces of evil and the accidents and fortunes of time and this world. What we cannot accept is that a figure who has been made supremely attractive on stage, with whom we are led to identify almost completely since he seems to anticipate and to surpass us in every way, should alienate us by both deciding and acting (upon whatever compulsion) to kill another in cold blood. He can, of course, kill any number of people upon impulse, when emotionally aroused: that is an understandable response which need not sacrifice our sympathies either on stage or off. He may kill hundreds in open warfare and numbers in duels, with opponents who can defend themselves and with the conventions open and recognized. But he cannot realistically plan a secret assassination, or stab someone in the back, or poison a supposedly innocuous drink, or cheat with an unbated and poisoned sword, or lunge instead of break after a fencing referee has rendered judgement.

> —Joseph H. Summers, "The Dream of a Hero: *Hamlet,*" *Dreams of Love and Power: On Shakespeare's Plays* (Oxford: Clarendon Press, 1984), pp. 58–60

Cedric Watts on the Many Interpretations of *Hamlet*

[Cedric Watts is a professor of English at the University of Texas. He has written *The Deceptive Text: An Introduction to Covert Plots* (1984), *A Preface to Keats* (1985), a study of *Romeo and Juliet* (1991), and several books on the British writer R. B. Cunninghame Graham. In this extract from his book on *Hamlet,* Watts maintains that the play is designed to yield many different critical interpretations and that there is no one view of the play that is "correct" to the exclusion of all others.]

What by now should be obvious is that *Hamlet* will tantalisingly offer cogent but not conclusive support to many different interpretations. For reasons of economy, vanity or ideology, critics are still rather reluctant to concede that there are many interesting and fruitful options; that the open secret of *Hamlet* is that it is so constituted as to invite, encourage and reward this diversity; and that its combination of order and muddle, of plenitude and reticence, of eloquent lucidity and silent opacity, denies final confirmation to any single interpretation. This is good, even lifelike, and not something to be feared. Criticism has too long been dominated by the struggle for the right approach, the best theory, the key to the mystery, the solution to the riddle. Critics of *Hamlet* need, perhaps, to relax into modesty and to turn from the pressure of competition to the pleasure of co-operation. *Hamlet* is generally rich, full, intelligent; clear in the main, dramatically satisfying; unclear in some features, providing plenty of scope for new interpretations on stage and film as well as in critical essays. It is protean partly by design (clever Shakespeare) and partly by accident (hasty Shakespeare). There is no master-*Hamlet* to be discovered by poring over the text, and we don't need such a discovery; yet we can hardly shrug our shoulders in resignation, for the pleasure of this play derives largely from our quest to solve its mysteries, to interrogate its ghost; and if we fail to seek what it never surrenders, we fail to enjoy what it renders. The value is that in our pursuit of answers, our search of the play is simultaneously a searching of life: an exploration of human identity, character, ethics, psychology, politics, what you will.

When we look into *Hamlet,* we tend to see ourselves reflected; and that's because the text has many mirrors built into it. The prince tells the actors that the purpose of playing is to 'hold, as 'twere, the mirror up to nature'; and the mirror of *Hamlet* is multiple, cracked and mobile, so that it pictures both past and future. If we and our preoccupations seem reflected in it, that is partly because the play has, to some degree, made us in its image: Shakespeare's perceptive eloquence has helped to generate future identities, future possibilities of living. We all contain more lives within ourselves than real life permits us to actualise; and Shakespeare proclaims these covert potentialities by generating from within himself a Polonius, an Ophelia, a Claudius, a Gertrude, and, most memorably of all, a Hamlet whose vitality so copiously exceeds all available roles.

—Cedric Watts, *Hamlet* (Boston: Twayne, 1988), pp. 79–80

T. MCALINDON ON LOVE IN *HAMLET*

[T. McAlindon (b. 1932) is Senior Lecturer in English at the University of Hull and author of *Shakespeare and Decorum* (1973), *English Renaissance Tragedy* (1976), and *Doctor Faustus: Divine in Show* (1994). In this extract from his 1991 book on Shakespeare, McAlindon believes that love is the guiding force behind many of Hamlet's actions.]

⟨. . .⟩ it is the intricate relationship between love and the call to violence and hatred that characterises Hamlet's tragic situation. Polonius is ironically correct when he declares that the cause of Hamlet's distraction is love: a passion 'Whose violent property fordoes itself / And leads the will to desperate undertakings' (II.i.103–4). We think of Hamlet as an embittered intellectual, but he is perhaps above all a man of warm and loving nature. His praise of Horatio is not the eulogy of a cool and cerebral type but that of a friend whose stability of nature makes his friendship all the more true. And it is part of a movingly tender exchange whose tone is set by Horatio's, 'Here, sweet lord', and 'O my dear lord' (III.ii.51, 53). Ophelia speaks of Hamlet's 'noble and most sovereign reason' but for her that was manifest in the eloquence of his love: in the honey of his musicked vows, in the gifts with such sweet breath composed as made the gifts more dear. Rosencrantz and Guildenstern are welcomed as 'good friends' and conjured by 'the rights of fellowship' and 'the obligation of . . . ever-preserved love' to speak truthfully (II.ii.223, 283–5). The soldiers and players too are the recipients of his 'love and friending' (I.v.186). From such evidence we infer the depth of Hamlet's love for his father and mother, his delight in the love they showed for each other, and the shock to his sensibility caused by his father's death and all that followed.

Fratricide is a primal symbol of the shattering of human bonds. And however hard it may be for us today to regard the marriage of Claudius to his sister-in-law as incestuous, it is presented exactly as ordinary forms of incest are treated in Middleton's *Women Beware Women* (c. 1621–5) and Ford's *'Tis Pity She's A Whore* (c. 1633): as a reflection of primal chaos where human bonds and the order of society may be said to begin. The stamp of deep confusion is imprinted on this marriage at the outset (although thereafter it seems one of genuine affection). Claudius publicly refers to Gertrude as 'our sometime sister, now our queen', and repeatedly addresses Hamlet as 'cousin and . . . son' (I.ii.7, 64, 117). For his part, Hamlet cannot comprehend how his mother would fail to distinguish between two brothers who seem as different to him as Hyperion and satyr (line 140), sunlit mountain and dark 'moor' (III.iv.67). Even more than fratricide and incest, however, the shallowness and inconstancy of his mother's love for his father horrifies Hamlet, causing him to confuse all women with her. Thus the virginal Ophelia is rejected as another potential whore and breeder of sinners. The brutality of Hamlet's verbal attacks on his mother and (especially) on Ophelia mark the depth of his confusion: this is where the tongue becomes a dagger, leading to violent death, madness, and (perhaps) suicide. And yet it is not a question of simple tranformation: for the verbal fury of the attack on Gertrude has a strongly moral component, and leads her to self-knowledge. And the obscene taunting of Ophelia is directly linked to wounded love: 'For look you how cheerfully my mother looks, and my father died within's two hours' (III.ii.121–3).

But if love drives Hamlet to the extreme point where opposites are deeply confused, it also seems to inhibit him there. The great hole in the middle of this play is the unwritten soliloquy in which Hamlet weighs the rights and wrongs of private revenge and identifies the cause of his delay. Hamlet's failure to do this testifies to the depth of his confusion. It has the added advantage of allowing Shakespeare to introduce a wide spectrum of moral and metaphysical questions as Hamlet's thoughts move round and about the predicament he does not understand. It also allows Shakespeare to suggest the force of that instinct which prevents Hamlet from becoming another Pyrrhus or Laertes in the quest for revenge.

Hamlet's state of confusion was signalled early on when he assured the ghost that he would sweep to his revenge 'with wings as swift / As meditation or the thoughts of love' (I.v.28–30): here he was proposing to confound with hatred and violence the two qualities which, in combination, distinguish him so clearly from the play's 'outstretch'd heroes'. But 'love' and 'meditation' themselves need distinguishing, for Hamlet's reflective capacity would not have saved him from the predicament into which the ghost and the unnatural brother have led him. In *Julius Caesar, King Lear,* and *Macbeth,* it is made clear that in times of great crisis the line between humanity and barbarism will be discerned, if at all, by 'the milk of human kindness', the capacity to 'see . . . feelingly'. Shakespeare intimates that when reason operates as it should in human relationships, it is following that instinct; when it is not (and most often it is not in the tragedies), it usually functions in plain opposition to it. That instinct, I assume, is responsible for the delay which Hamlet's reason cannot account for.

Support for this interpretation can be found in Shakespeare's attitude to fear. Echoing the code of honour, Hamlet indicts himself of cowardice and assumes that fear frustrates not only his own revenge but also many other heroic enterprises of great moment (II.ii.565–72; III.i.83–8; IV.iv.43). He is right to accuse himself of fear but quite wrong in his understanding of it. As will become much more obvious in *Macbeth,* but is apparent also in *Troilus and Cressida,* Shakespeare sees fear as an important element in the rational humanity which keeps heroic endeavour from going beyond the pale; it is allied to pity and human kindness and it is at the very heart of what we call 'conscience'. In the council scene where Troilus equates reason with cowardice and dishonour, Hector contends that 'modest doubt' is 'the beacon of the wise', and explains that fear can be a form of sensitivity which begets rational speculation about the consequences in terms of human life of every martial undertaking (*Troilus and Cressida* II.ii.11–15). So in *Hamlet* the 'pale cast of thought'—the fearful irresolution that is a conventional attribute of the melancholy man—is, by implication, doing what 'the pales and forts of reason' would normally be expected to do.

—T. McAlindon, *Shakespeare's Tragic Cosmos* (Cambridge: Cambridge University Press, 1991), pp. 111–13

[Zulfikar Ghose (b. 1935) is a noted Pakistani novelist, poet, and critic. Among his novels are *The Contradictions* (1966) and *The Murder of Aziz Khan* (1967). He has written an autobiography, *Confessions of a Native-Alien* (1965), and several critical studies, including *Hamlet, Prufrock, and Language* (1978) and *Shakespeare's Mortal Knowledge* (1993), from which this extract is taken. Here, Ghose studies the character of Ophelia and asserts that her "madness" is an indication of the visionary truth she has seen but is unable to express.]

Ophelia has gone mad and the Queen says: 'I will not speak with her'.

One cannot speak with the mad, they talk a different language; one does not wish to hear them either, they might utter something so mad that it is a revelation of truth. And the Queen has already been battered by words: she had to beg Hamlet to *speak no more,* for she had believed him to be mad and his enraged language had suddenly revealed him as both sane and in possession of truths she had not wanted to confront, and here is Ophelia who is decidely mad and God knows what she might not say. No. *I will not speak with her.* The Queen is terrified of words.

> GENTLEMAN: She is importunate, indeed distract.

As was Hamlet in Act I when he saw his father's Ghost and called to him importunately, 'O, answer me! / Let me not burst in ignorance . . . ' . The Gentleman then says of Ophelia that she

> . . . says she hears
> There's tricks i' th' world . . .

that she 'speaks things in doubt' and that

> Her speech is nothing,
> Yet the unshapèd use of it doth move
> The hearers to collection; they aim at it,
> And botch the words up fit to their own thoughts,

and while it is certain that there is nothing in her words there is nevertheless much there, 'unhappily'. A language that conveys nothing is still conveying the idea that language can be used to express no meaning. And sometimes a meaningless language (as, for example, of literary criticism) is heard as conveying significance because we 'botch the words up', interpret them, according to an established intellectual prejudice. There is no understanding that does not make a cross reference to belief.

Ophelia's madness is *heard* in her speeches and her songs; it pours into the ears of her hearers as had the poison into the ear of the King asleep in the garden. She whose language had no responsible relationship with reality but went about giving an impression of logical speech has now abandoned the world of appearances. Something in her mind tells her that there are tricks in the world, and these are not only deceptions which she has experienced, finding herself cheated of the happiness she had expected, but also deceptions to do with her understanding of the world itself: she has arrived at Hamlet's perception but not having Hamlet's rational language can make nothing of it: *Her speech is nothing,* her words are 'nothing worth'. And when Laertes sees her later in the scene, he says, 'This nothing's more than matter'. It is matter itself, this *Nothing.*

And when she enters, she utters a simple truth in her madness: she sings, and the imagery of her songs is to do with death and procreation. The mad are seen to have reverted to some prelapsarian innocence; our pity for them is mingled with an awe and sometimes, as with a John Clare, we consider them sentimentally as divinely blessed. Ophelia sings with a poet's simple beauty:

> He is dead and gone, lady,
>   He is dead and gone;
> At his head a grass-green turf,
>   At his heels a stone.

Or she can be bawdy:

Then up he rose and donned his clo'es
   And dupped the chamber door,
Let in the maid, that out a maid
   Never departed more.

But all the visionary truth that her madness can reveal is to do with breeding and dying. The quest for meaning has been eliminated: there is no 'before and after' for the mad.

She breaks off her song to say, 'Lord, we know what we are, but know not what we may be'. And 'Pray let's have no words of this'. She is the only one who can say with perfect conviction that *we know what we are,* but the language with which she reveals this is of 'unshaped use': her hearers can understand her only intuitively but are convinced that there is nothing to understand. *Pray let's have no words of this,* let us listen to the song. The philosopher ends with silence, the poet dies singing.

—Zulfikar Ghose, Shakespeare's Mortal Knowledge: A Reading of the Tragedies (Basingstoke, UK: Macmillan Press, 1993), pp. 58–60

KAY STANTON ON "GET THEE TO A NUNNERY"

[Kay Stanton is a professor of English at California State University at Fullerton and author of articles on Shakespeare, Christopher Marlowe, and John Milton. In the following extract, Stanton examines Hamlet's derisive statement to Ophelia, "Get thee to a nunnery" (which really means, "Go to a whorehouse"), finding that it is emblematic of the male characters' attitude toward the women in the play.]

'Get thee to a nunnery' (III. i. 121): in a play filled with memorable lines, this has been one of the most often quoted. As editors rarely fail to note in gloss, 'nunnery' was Elizabethan slang for 'brothel', so Hamlet *really* tells Ophelia to go to a whorehouse, where, he believes, she belongs. Why does the virtuous

Ophelia belong, in Hamlet's judgement, in a whorehouse? A frequent answer has been that Hamlet so relegates her because of his disillusionment with women resulting from the revelation of his mother's lustfulness; *Gertrude* belongs in a whorehouse, since she has been 'whor'd' by Claudius (V. ii. 64). Because Gertrude has become a whore, so will Ophelia—and so, in fact, will all women, in the estimation not only of Hamlet but also of those many men of various generations who have quoted—I would say prostituted—the line for the purpose of smugly concurring (and implying Shakespeare's concurrence) with Hamlet's estimation of woman's whorish nature.

A slightly more sophisticated reading of the passage in which the line occurs might recognize that both meanings of 'nunnery' are operating: Ophelia is too virtuous for this corrupt world, which will prostitute her to its ways if she does not retreat into a cloistered religious life. Hamlet is 'cruel only to be kind' (III. iv. 180). The world will corrupt Ophelia as it has corrupted Gertrude; Gertrude has become a whore, a fate that Hamlet wishes Ophelia to avoid, so he must therefore shock her, even by denying his feelings of love. This reading, however, still leaves Gertrude a whore, but it does also neatly reflect another comfortable misogynistic position that the play's commentators have often pandered it to: not all women are whores; some are Madonnas. Certainly the play as reflected through the male characters' perceptions seems to support this position. Women in *Hamlet* are allowed by the play's men to have two and only two choices: virgin or whore. Ophelia cannot, but Hamlet can, be 'indifferent honest' (III. i. 122). So far as the play provides evidence, Gertrude has indulged in sexual activity only in marriage, yet even legalized expression of sexuality merits her the label of 'whore': she suffers from the 'plague' that Hamlet gives Ophelia for *her* dowry: 'be thou as chaste as ice, as pure as snow, thou shalt not escape calumny' (III. i. 136–8). Thus the second position on women doubles back into the first: there may seem to be two choices for women of virgin or whore, but if a woman tries to be virtuous *and* sexual in monogamous marriage, or even if a woman remains an unmarried virgin, she cannot escape the 'calumny' that will brand her a whore: all women are thus whores, either by action or by slander.

Of course, although it seems to warn against slander from others, the passage is itself an exercise in such 'calumny': Ophelia's honour is verbally violated by Hamlet in his speech— and it may have already been done so in action: he may indeed have raped her in the offstage closet interlude that she reports, perhaps only in part, to her father in II. i. 75–110. The onstage Hamlet-woman-closet scene in III. iv. is usually staged, with good reason, to simulate a rape by Hamlet of Gertrude. If both Gertrude and Ophelia are whores, it is Hamlet himself who has made them so, in words if not deeds, by *his* calumny. Although the other male characters may be seen to share Hamlet's misogyny, no male character not named 'Hamlet', elder or younger, *calls* either woman a whore.

Perhaps it may be granted, however, that what makes a woman a whore in the Hamlets' estimation is her sexual use not by one man but by more than one man: Gertrude seems not to have been a whore in old Hamlet's judgement until she bedded Claudius; Ophelia, even if she has been sexually used by young Hamlet, is not seen by him as a whore until she has been employed as a sex object by Polonius, her 'fishmonger' (II. ii. 174), or pimp. The rape of Ophelia by Hamlet may be more verbal than physical; the pandering of Ophelia by her father is more symbolic than literal, so its interpretation may be missed by the naive. Though I would concur with Hamlet that Polonius employs Ophelia's sexuality for his purposes, Polonius seems not to see himself as a 'fishmonger', and Ophelia certainly does not see herself as a whore—it is, again, primarily Hamlet's interpretation that makes them so, and, as he states later in the scene, 'there is nothing either good or bad but thinking makes it so' (II. ii. 249–50).

—Kay Stanton, "*Hamlet's* Whores," *New Essays on* Hamlet, ed. Mark Thornton Burnett and John Manning (New York: AMS Press, 1994), pp. 167–69

Works by
William Shakespeare

Venus and Adonis. 1593.
The Rape of Lucrece. 1594.
Henry VI. 1594.
Titus Andronicus. 1594.
The Taming of the Shrew. 1594.
Romeo and Juliet. 1597.
Richard III. 1597.
Richard II. 1597.
Love's Labour's Lost. 1598.
Henry IV. 1598.
The Passionate Pilgrim. 1599.
A Midsummer Night's Dream. 1600.
The Merchant of Venice. 1600.
Much Ado about Nothing. 1600.
Henry V. 1600.
The Phoenix and the Turtle. 1601.
The Merry Wives of Windsor. 1602.
Hamlet. 1603.
King Lear. 1608.
Troilus and Cressida. 1609.
Sonnets. 1609.
Pericles. 1609.
Othello. 1622.
Mr. William Shakespeare's Comedies, Histories & Tragedies. Ed. John Heminge and Henry Condell. 1623 (First Folio), 1632 (Second Folio), 1663 (Third Folio), 1685 (Fourth Folio).
Poems. 1640.
Works. Ed. Nicholas Rowe. 1709. 6 vols.
Works. Ed. Alexander Pope. 1723–25. 6 vols.
Works. Ed. Lewis Theobald. 1733. 7 vols.
Works. Ed. Thomas Hanmer. 1743–44. 6 vols.
Works. Ed. William Warburton. 1747. 8 vols.
Plays. Ed. Samuel Johnson. 1765. 8 vols.
Plays and Poems. Ed. Edmond Malone. 1790. 10 vols.
The Family Shakespeare. Ed. Thomas Bowdler. 1807. 4 vols.
Works. Ed. J. Payne Collier. 1842–44. 8 vols.
Works. Ed. H. N. Hudson. 1851–56. 11 vols.
Works. Ed. Alexander Dyce. 1857. 6 vols.
Works. Ed. Richard Grant White. 1857–66. 12 vols.

Works (Cambridge Edition). Ed. William George Clark, John Glover, and William Aldis Wright. 1863–66. 9 vols.

A New Variorum Edition of the Works of Shakespeare. Ed. H. H. Furness et al. 1871– .

Works. Ed. W. J. Rolfe. 1871–96. 40 vols.

The Pitt Press Shakespeare. Ed. A. W. Verity. 1890–1905. 13 vols.

The Warwick Shakespeare. 1893–1938. 13 vols.

The Temple Shakespeare. Ed. Israel Gollancz. 1894–97. 40 vols.

The Arden Shakespeare. Ed. W. J. Craig, R. H. Case et al. 1899–1924. 37 vols.

The Shakespeare Apocrypha. Ed. C. F. Tucker Brooke. 1908.

The Yale Shakespeare. Ed. Wilbur L. Cross, Tucker Brooke, and Willard Highley Durham. 1917–27. 40 vols.

The New Shakespeare (Cambridge Edition). Ed. Arthur Quiller-Couch and John Dover Wilson. 1921–62. 38 vols.

The New Temple Shakespeare. Ed. M. R. Ridley. 1934–36. 39 vols.

Works. Ed. George Lyman Kittredge. 1936.

The Penguin Shakespeare. Ed. G. B. Harrison. 1937–59. 36 vols.

The New Clarendon Shakespeare. Ed. R. E. C. Houghton. 1938– .

The Arden Shakespeare. Ed. Una Ellis-Fermor et al. 1951– .

The Complete Pelican Shakespeare. Ed. Alfred Harbage. 1969.

The Complete Signet Classic Shakespeare. Ed. Sylvan Barnet. 1972.

The Oxford Shakespeare. Ed. Stanley Wells. 1982– .

The New Cambridge Shakespeare. Ed. Philip Brockbank. 1984– .

Works about William Shakespeare and Hamlet

Andrews, John F., ed. *William Shakespeare: His World, His Work, His Influence.* New York: Scribner's, 1985. 3 vols.

Bayley, John. *Shakespeare and Tragedy.* London: Routledge & Kegan Paul, 1981.

Berkoff, Steven. *I Am Hamlet.* New York: Grove Weidenfeld, 1990.

Bolt, Sydney. *William Shakespeare,* Hamlet. London: Penguin, 1990.

Bulman, James C. *The Heroic Idiom of Shakespearean Tragedy.* Newark: University of Delaware Press, 1985.

Calderwood, James. *To Be and Not to Be: Negation and Metadrama in* Hamlet. New York: Columbia University Press, 1983.

Cantor, Paul A. *Shakespeare,* Hamlet. Cambridge: Cambridge University Press, 1989.

Charlton, H. B. *Shakespearian Tragedy.* Cambridge: Cambridge University Press, 1948.

Charney, Maurice. *Hamlet's Fictions.* London: Routledge & Kegan Paul, 1987.

Dollimore, Jonathan. *Radical Tragedy: Religion, Ideology, and Power in the Drama of Shakespeare and His Contemporaries.* Chicago: University of Chicago Press, 1984.

Empson, William. "When Hamlet Was New." *Sewanee Review* 61 (1953): 15–42, 185–205.

Erickson, Peter. *Patriarchal Structures in Shakespeare's Drama.* Berkeley: University of California Press, 1985.

Farnham, Willard. *Shakespeare's Tragic Frontier: The World of His Final Tragedies.* Berkeley: University of California Press, 1950.

Felperin, Howard. *Shakespearean Representation.* Princeton: Princeton University Press, 1977.

Foakes, R. A. *Hamlet versus Lear: Cultural Politics and Shakespeare's Art.* Cambridge: Cambridge University Press, 1993.

Frye, Northrop. *Fools of Time: Studies in Shakespearean Tragedy.* Toronto: University of Toronto Press, 1967.

Furtwangler, Albert. *Assassin on Stage: Brutus, Hamlet, and the Death of Lincoln.* Urbana: University of Illinois Press, 1991.

Goldberg, Jonathan. "Hamlet's Hand." *Shakespeare Quarterly* 39 (1988): 307–27.

Goldman, Michael. *Acting and Action in Shakespearean Tragedy.* Princeton: Princeton University Press, 1985.

Hobson, Alan. *Full Circle: Shakespeare and Moral Development.* London: Chatto & Windus, 1972.

Holland, Norman N. *The Shakespearean Imagination.* New York: Macmillan, 1964.

Holloway, John. *The Story of the Night: Studies in Shakespeare's Major Tragedies.* London: Routledge & Kegan Paul, 1961.

Jenkins, Harold. *Hamlet and Ophelia.* Oxford: Oxford University Press, 1964.

Jones, Emrys. *Scenic Form in Shakespeare.* Oxford: Clarendon Press, 1971.

Kermode, Frank. *Shakespeare, Spenser, Donne.* London: Routledge & Kegan Paul, 1971.

Kerrigan, William. *Hamlet's Perfection.* Baltimore: Johns Hopkins University Press, 1994.

Knight, G. Wilson. *Shakespeare's Dramatic Challenge: On the Rise of Shakespeare's Tragic Heroes.* London: Croom Helm; New York: Barnes & Noble, 1977.

Knights, L. C. *An Approach to* Hamlet. London: Chatto & Windus, 1960.

———. *Hamlet and Other Shakespearean Essays.* Cambridge: Cambridge University Press, 1979.

Kott, Jan. "Hamlet and Orestes." Tr. Boleslaw Taborski. *PMLA* 82 (1967): 303–13.

Lacan, Jacques. "Desire and the Interpretation of Desire in *Hamlet*." Tr. James Hulbert. *Yale French Studies* Nos. 55–56 (1977): 11–52.

Levin, Harry. *The Question of Hamlet*. Oxford: Oxford University Press, 1959.

Lawlor, John. *The Tragic Sense in Shakespeare*. London: Chatto & Windus, 1960.

McAlindon, T. *Shakespeare and Decorum*. London: Macmillan, 1973.

McElroy, Bernard. *Shakespeare's Mature Tragedies*. Princeton: Princeton University Press, 1973.

Mack, Maynard, Jr. *Killing the King: Three Studies in Shakespeare's Tragic Structure*. New Haven: Yale University Press, 1973.

McGee, Arthur. *The Elizabethan* Hamlet. New Haven: Yale University Press, 1987.

Mangan, Michael. *A Preface to Shakespeare's Tragedies*. London: Longman, 1991.

Margolies, David. *Monsters of the Deep: Social Dissolution in Shakespeare's Tragedies*. Manchester, UK: Manchester University Press, 1992.

Morris, Ivor. *Shakespeare's God: The Role of Religion in the Tragedies*. London: George Allen & Unwin, 1972.

Muir, Kenneth. *Shakespeare's Tragic Sequence*. New York: Barnes & Noble, 1979.

Nardo, Anna K. "Hamlet, 'A Man to Double Business Bound.'" *Shakespeare Quarterly* 34 (1983): 181–99.

Nevo, Ruth. *Tragic Form in Shakespeare*. Princeton: Princeton University Press, 1972.

Newell, Axel. *The Soliloquies in* Hamlet: *The Structural Design*. Rutherford, NJ: Fairleigh Dickinson University Press, 1991.

Prosner, Matthew N. *The Heroic Image in Five Shakespearean Tragedies*. Princeton: Princeton University Press, 1965.

Robinson, D. W. "A Medievalist Looks at Hamlet." In Robinson's *Essays in Medieval Culture.* Princeton: Princeton University Press, 1980, pp. 312–31.

Rosen, William. *Shakespeare and the Craft of Tragedy.* Cambridge, MA: Harvard University Press, 1960.

Russell, John. *Hamlet and Narcissus.* London: Associated University Presses, 1995.

Ryan, Kiernan. *Shakespeare.* Atlantic Highlands, NJ: Humanities Press, 1989.

Sanders, Wilbur. *The Dramatist and the Received Idea: Studies in the Plays of Marlowe and Shakespeare.* Cambridge: Cambridge University Press, 1968.

Sewell, Arthur. *Character and Society in Shakespeare.* Oxford: Clarendon Press, 1951.

Smidt, Kristian. *Unconformities in Shakespeare's Tragedies.* New York: St. Martin's Press, 1990.

Smith, Molly. *The Darker World Within: Evil in the Tragedies of Shakespeare and His Successors.* Newark: University of Delaware Press, 1991.

States, Bert O. *Hamlet and the Concept of Character.* Baltimore: Johns Hopkins University Press, 1992.

Stockholder, Kay. *Dream Works: Lovers and Families in Shakespeare's Plays.* Toronto: University of Toronto Press, 1987.

Sypher, Wylie. *The Ethic of Time: Structures of Experience in Shakespeare.* New York: Seabury Press, 1976.

Wilson, Dover. *What Happens in* Hamlet. Cambridge: Cambridge University Press, 1935.

Wilson, Harold S. *On the Design of Shakespearean Tragedy.* Toronto: University of Toronto Press, 1957.

Index of
Themes and Ideas